Recipe *for* Disaster

Recipe *for* Disaster

40 SUPERSTAR STORIES OF SUSTENANCE AND SURVIVAL

Alison Riley

CHRONICLE BOOKS
SAN FRANCISCO

Library of Congress Cataloging-in-
Publication Data available.

ISBN 978-1-7972-1282-1

Manufactured in China.

MIX
Paper | Supporting
responsible forestry
FSC™ C008047

Design by Ben Wagner.
Typesetting by Sam Wagner.

Typeset in Minion Pro (Adobe Fonts,
Robert Slimbach), Victor Serif (Kometa),
and Mrs Eaves (Emigre, Zuzana Licko).

10 9 8 7 6 5 4 3 2 1

Chronicle books and gifts are
available at special quantity discounts
to corporations, professional
associations, literacy programs,
and other organizations. For details
and discount information, please
contact our premiums department at
corporatesales@chroniclebooks.com
or at 1-800-759-0190.

Chronicle Books LLC
680 Second Street
San Francisco, California 94107
www.chroniclebooks.com

For my dad, who I always thought was the author of the world's best hollandaise recipe, only to discover it came with our Cuisinart. Here's to you and me, and all the disasters behind us.

Contents

Introduction   12

Samantha Irby *Rejection Chicken*   18

Sarah Silverman *In Bed with No Fever*   22

Hannah Black and Carla Perez-Gallardo *Under the Sea*   25

Bowen Yang *Seasoned, Not Sauced*   31

Michael W. Twitty ODDBALL   32

Alice Waters *Without a Gathering, a Good Salad*   36

Laurie Woolever *The Best of the Worst*   41

Cey Adams *Portrait of a Single Father*   44

Chelsea Peretti *Pesto to Pass Time*   49

Tien Nguyen *A Balm Then, a Balm Now*   52

Joan As Police Woman *Forget All Your Troubles*   57

Hassan Pierre *A Mess for a Moment*   60

Nicholas Galanin *Coasting in on an Empty Tank*   64

Bob Power *To Accompany Pig*   68

Money Mark *The Art of Giving*   72

Kia Cooks *How to Treat Yourself*   77

Simon Doonan *A Ritual of Hope*   80

Liz Lambert *Beans for All Time*   85

Justin Vivian Bond *Crispy, Hot, Salty Potatoes*   89

Meshell Ndegeocello *For the Record*   92

Alex Wagner *A Soft Spot*   97

Ulla Johnson *Amidst a City Torn Apart*   100

Bobbito García
aka Kool Bob Love *When the Rims Went Down*   105

LinYee Yuan *The Simplicity of Congee*   108

Brian Lehrer *Indestructible Pea Soup*   112

Gabrielle Hamilton *A G&T for the Down & Out*   117

Richard Christiansen *If Martha Stewart Only Knew!*   121

Fran Tirado *Scared & Horny Sandwich*   124

Becca Blackwell *Security Pizza*   128

Rachel McKibbens *Staples*   132

Jacqueline Woodson *Mother of Invention*   137

Raul Lopez *Zigni to Warm My Heart*   140

Alba Clemente *Joy and Relief*   143

Damani Baker *A Dish to Hold the Love*   144

Ron Finley *Spread Peanut Butter, Not Pain*   148

Thundercat *My Favorite, Then and Now*   153

Angelo Baque *Ceviche on the Stoop*   154

Andrew Tarlow *An Overflow of Love and Plumbing*   158

Kyle Abraham *Eighth Grade Memory Dance*   163

Emily King *De-Humiliating Muffins*   167

Acknowledgments   172

Introduction

While I am quite fluent in disasters, when it comes to cooking I am a person who needs a recipe. I do not possess the ability to throw things together to make a magical meal. Many of my friends and family members are alchemists of that kind, combining disparate ingredients from various cabinets in a way they just have a hunch might be complimentary. I have none of that. When I inquire about how somebody's chicken was prepared or a stew was created and they tell me to use a little turmeric, some shallots, throw in a chili pepper, or a bit of white wine, I know I am never going to make whatever they're describing. I need cold, hard measurements and instructions.

Though my creativity does not extend to the kitchen, much of my memory is punctuated by food. Pizelles my grandmother made at Christmas. My mother's baguettes that I loved and the ziti salad I never liked. Steak and cheese subs with my best friend in high school. Kimchi from care packages received by my college roommate. Oysters in Provincetown. Kofta in Marrakesh. Collards at home. While my wife was out of town for a long stretch, our son wrote a letter to her that was solely about how much he missed her tacos. Food is integral to our emotional lives, but while we plan, choose, and prepare special things when we revel and commemorate, on those days when there is less to celebrate, we still have to eat.

I embarked on this project with an idea of the humor and heartache it might yield, but hearing the stories people were generous enough to share brought the point of this project into real focus. This book is meant to remind us of the value of our experiences, both good and bad, and to bring levity and purpose to the moments we need them most. It was conceived through the deeply held belief that there is liberation and universal truth to be found through the exchange of *all* stories, even those full of sorrow, fear, or loneliness. From flat tires to pet deaths to unbearable losses, *Recipe for Disaster* aims to remember, without hierarchy or judgment, that our lowest moments offer something worth sharing: stories, food, and the welcome reminder that we've all been there.

In contemplating an example of my own, many stories came to mind. The first was a spectacularly catastrophic breakup, in the course of which there was fire and people died, and after which I was living alone in an apartment where I was used to sharing the rent. Between being sad, broke, and cooking illiterate, I made the same thing for dinner every night for months: steamed tofu and frozen spinach with sesame oil, tamari, and black sesame seeds alongside one slice of toast with Tofutti cream cheese. At the time,

I felt victorious as I prepared it because I was doing something for myself, not spending a lot of money, and not eating unhealthy things. I was comforted by the predictability and repetition of the ritual. It was like a meditation, or a quiet, daily promise to push forward and take care of myself. I know I stopped making this meal as the weather turned cold, about four or five months later, but I can't really say why. I don't think I was fully recovered from the heartbreak, but maybe I was sure I eventually would be.

A decade later, I contracted Lyme disease without knowing it and was not diagnosed until I was over a year into the infection. By then, I could barely move my arms and legs and could not buckle my own seat belt or button a shirt. I dressed myself in the evenings when I had slightly more mobility and then slept in my clothes, so I could use all my strength in the morning to dress my toddler for preschool. It was a wild and terrifying time. The infection eventually gave way to rheumatoid arthritis, and I adopted a strict anti-inflammatory diet to avoid the scariest medications and manage my symptoms. Eventually, my RA went into remission. This is a rather extreme version of a "recipe," but this was as low a point as I can recall, and food came to my rescue in a most literal way.

Many of the people who contributed to this book said that writing or talking with me about their stories was cathartic. Hearing them proved to be as well. I aspire to be like Ron Finley, who doesn't see memory as positive or negative. I can only hope to be as resilient as Laurie Woolever or as loyal to lost friends as Simon Doonan and Thundercat. I hope Samantha Irby's story gives us all permission to embrace what might feel embarrassing and offer it to others, rendering it powerless over any of us and empowering to us all. The responses to my question "Can you name a low point, of any size and shape, and the food memory you associate with surviving it?" are diverse in every way, but each of them feels unexpected and all of them comforting. People shared stories with me that they often had not otherwise shared at all. Beyond a map out of grief, beyond a collection of tales from interesting thinkers, that was the point: to surface what usually stays buried, however profound or pedestrian. To me, all of it is worth celebrating.

If nothing else, I hope this book proves that we are all dealt lemons. Collecting and sharing these stories is my version of lemonade.

—Alison Riley

Rejection Chicken by Samantha Irby

WRITER

1. First things first, you gotta get dumped. Everybody gets dumped! I have been broken up with dozens of times, mostly for reasons that I refuse to believe are my fault, and every single time the feeling I get afterward isn't sadness or despair or unrequited longing… it's hunger. I'm sure a more poetic person could come up with an analogy equating hunger and emotional emptiness or something, but I don't talk like that. I eat my feelings. I have a lot of feelings, and I eat them, especially when the feeling in question is LIKE PURE SHIT. So you've been rejected, you're some gross combination of mad and/or sad about it, but you still need to eat. Go to the store to get ice cream and also grab:

    INGREDIENTS

    1 pack of chicken thighs (get a pound?)

    Ground cinnamon

    Curry powder

    Olive oil

    1 yellow onion

    4 zucchini

    Pepper and the dehydrated salt from your tears

    2 cups [480 ml] of cream

    One 32 oz [960 ml] box of chicken broth

    Jasmine rice or leftover take-out rice or whatever rice-adjacent foodstuff you enjoy

    Fresh basil (if you are fancy)

    A pack of slivered almonds

2. Okay, now that we're ready to cook, the first thing you have to do is put on your sad playlist. I make very specific playlists for myself, and the theme of 95 percent of them is "cool funeral." I'd recommend blasting the saddest songs you can think of from a speaker, but before I got one, I would just throw my phone in a coffee cup to amplify the sound, and you know what? That's fine, who cares! Pairing a Bluetooth on shitty Wi-Fi is torture, so skip it.

3. Cut the chicken into chunks and put them in a large bowl. Cutting up slimy dead meat is a yucky feeling that I ordinarily avoid, but I *promise* having to saw through those weird fatty white strings and the occasional bloody piece with your dull, regular-person knives is worth it, or, at the very least, will distract you from your malaise for at least a few minutes. If you're really goth,

cont.

you can pretend it's one of your ex's tender vital organs. Once it's all cut up, uncap both your cinnamon and your curry powder and liberally shake them over the chicken. Stir the pieces or flip them over using whatever tool feels practical to you to coat them evenly, then set the bowl aside.

4.   Put your cast-iron Dutch oven on the stovetop, turn the heat on low, and put a couple glugs of olive oil in the pan. A thing you need to know about me is that I have no idea what differentiates good olive oil from bad, and I have absolutely zero interest in learning. This is a meal you are going to eat on the toilet while you weep, so it truly does not matter if your olive oil came from the garbage. Okay, so you're heating your pan and your oil on the lowest heat setting, and while that magic happens you're going to slice your onion however you like onions to be sliced, and drop them in the pan. As they start sizzling, wash your zucchini, cut the ends off, then I like to slice them on a severe angle because it looks cool and chef-y, but honestly? It doesn't matter! Does anything?????? Once the zucchini are sliced up, drop them in the pan with the onion and the hot oil, stir to coat, and turn the heat up a touch.

5.   Are you feeling like a cook now? This is the part where I look around the kitchen, thrilled by the sounds and the smells and low-key in awe that I am the one making those things happen, and break my fucking arm trying to pat myself on the back. But we're not done! Season the zucchini and onions with lots of salt and pepper as they cook, and as things start to soften a bit, dump in your chicken chunks and another glug of olive oil if shit is looking dry. Stir everything again and don't worry—the cinnamon/curry mixture might look a little muddy, but trust me, it's fine.

6.   Now is a good time, while the chicken cooks, to unfollow your ex on social media and block their phone number. I mean, unless they need to coordinate picking up the bike they left in your front hall or whatever, why would you need to hear from them? Keep an eye on the pan as you drop their follower count from seventy-four to seventy-three, and when the chicken gets kinda bouncy (I am not sure which adjective I should use instead of this one, so hopefully it's clear what I mean) and cooked-looking, pour the entire pint of cream into the pan.

7. Technically, you could stop here. You could heat the cream through and season it to taste and just be done with it. And if that's where you're at? I respect it. I like to make it slightly less rich—i.e., add some mildly flavored water to it so that it makes more sauce and I can stretch it over a couple of days. So, I pour in an entire box of broth and bring it to a slow boil, then let it simmer for a little while so the flavors can meld. And while that alchemy is happening, I make a pot of rice, and I will not insult you by assuming you don't know how to do that.

8. When your rice is done and your rejection chicken (sad person curry!) is hot, season to taste with salt and pepper, then sprinkle some basil on it and throw handfuls of slivered almonds in it, serve it over scoops of hot rice in the biggest bowl you feel comfortable crawling into bed with, and eat and eat and eat until that deep well of sadness inside you is filled with chicken and nuts and cream. Then, delete all of your cutie little text threads and throw out the old anniversary cards and wash your face and go to bed. And there will still be some left when you wake up starving and sobbing over that moron (I know, I get it) tomorrow.

In Bed with No Fever by Sarah Silverman

COMEDIAN

I was thirteen the first time I experienced long-term clinical depression. It came over me as fast as a cloud covers the sun. As fast as when you are fine one moment and the next you're like, "Oh fuck, I have the flu." It was my first experience with depression, my first experience with having monumental, cellular-level change that happens in an instant. There was no cinematic slow motion telling me, "This is big." No music tipping me off to trauma. It just . . . happened. And suddenly, my perspective had shifted—maybe just one single degree, but the whole world looked different.

I went from being a social butterfly to not wanting to be with or talk to anyone. Not even my identical twin best friend. I loved school, and now I couldn't bear to go. I missed three straight months of school for reasons I couldn't articulate. I stayed in a ball in bed with no fever, no cough, no physicalization of un-wellness.

And just one sensory joy. Pinwheels. Chocolate-covered marshmallow cookies. When I see them at the grocery store now, they make me so sad for that little New Hampshire kid who didn't know what was wrong with her. But they were my salvation.

Under the Sea by Hannah Black and Carla Perez-Gallardo

FOUNDING PARTNERS OF LIL DEB'S OASIS

Our restaurant has a vibey, buzzy energy on a regular night, but for New Year's Eve, we like to take it to the next level. There is always a theme that involves costumes, decor, a playlist, *and* a complex multicourse dinner menu that is conceptually aligned. We are ambitious, to say the least. Every December 31, over the course of our three seatings, there is a very hard and fast learning curve as we figure out these new dishes and service styles in real time, in front of our live audience of paying customers.

Our third annual New Year's Eve party, *Under the Sea*, stands out the most. Naturally, we crafted a seafood-focused multicourse meal, and our staff were all dressed as sea creatures, mermaids, and divers. Green and blue crepe streamers were hanging from the ceiling as waves and algae. The first turn was rough; there were a lot of kinks to work out. We had ambitiously put a squid-ink paella on the menu as our main course and had not had a lot of time to test the timing, so the food wasn't coming out as fast as it should. The 6 p.m. block of NYE diners is always a little awkward—it's just too early. But we made it through more or less on time, and the people left happy.

Now time for the second turn. We were ready, kinks ironed out, *bring it on!* As our first customers for the 8 p.m. seating sat down, we felt confident that we had everything under control. The lights were dim, the kitchen was humming, and the music was bumping. Until . . . *drip, drip*, our lead line cook felt a few droplets of an unidentified liquid on their head. *Drip, drip.* "What the fuck is that!?" we thought in sheer panic, quickly assuring the customers sitting in direct view that there was not a bathroom directly above. We darted upstairs, to our private dining room, where some of our staff had been setting up the illegal bar for our overflow. There was our culprit. A boxed wine, a silver bladder containing the equivalent of three bottles, had accidentally burst and there was organic tempranillo flowing everywhere and dripping down through the floorboards. Could be worse.

We joked with our customers that here at Lil' Deb's Oasis it rains wine, cleaned up the mess, and proceeded to move on with the 8 p.m. seating, applying what we learned in the first turn to ensure a smoother service.

Finally it's time, the 10 p.m. seating, the most special of them all! We rush to clean and reset the tables of the previous guests, knowing that we are running a little behind. The goal is to get the desserts out before midnight, and we are racing against the clock. We have confidence that this will be the smoothest and most fun of the three seatings—after all, the real fun begins after the clock strikes midnight. But nay. Reports start coming back from our servers: One table is saying that they are full after the first course, another table is barely eating, another table is just a bit odd. Everyone seemed to be thoroughly enjoying themselves, no one seemed particularly perturbed, no food was sent back, but the kitchen was frustrated. We finally had it! This was gonna be good! Why was nobody eating? Slowly it dawned on us: Nearly half the restaurant was tripping on mushrooms (usually the 10 p.m. seating is full of our friends, so that checks out). Everyone was just really, really high. Too high to eat our delicious, lovingly prepared meal.

Eventually midnight rolled around, and dessert had not yet been sent out. We got into our positions anyway, mounting the bar to release the celebratory confetti cannons. "5, 4, 3, 2, 1, HAPPY NEW YEAR!!!!!" All the fish and mermaids, lobsters and deep sea divers hugged and kissed each other, many of them deep in the trenches of a psychedelic journey. We went around and offered dessert to anyone who wanted it, but there was no going back—the party had begun, and tables were cleared to make room for the dance floor. It was a brand-new year.

This year was a particularly new dawn, as it was the last service before a major renovation project began in our space. We had been grinding it out for the previous three years in an incredibly small and dysfunctional space. This was our final hurrah, our goodbye to the old and a welcoming into our glow-up. We partied hard that night, crepe paper confetti mixing with squid ink rice, sticking to the bottom of our platform heels. A group of close friends gathered in our kitchen, a space that we lovingly referred to as a "shithole" (there was a literal hole in the floor, so . . .), to pay our respects to the past and say our goodbyes. We laughed and cried in near disbelief at how far we had come. Eventually, a particularly drunk and expressive gesture was followed by a large crash. Three entire racks of freshly

Nearly half
the restaurant
was tripping
on mushrooms.

washed glasses, stacked precariously on the edge of a lowboy, had fallen to the floor. Glass shards everywhere, the floor beyond filthy. That was a sign: It was time to go. We closed up shop, and the next week, the entire kitchen was demolished.

It was three long months until we were able to reopen. As the saying goes, construction always takes twice as long and is twice as expensive as you'd expect. We were cleaning up dried squid ink rice until the day we reopened. It really gets everywhere.

Squid Ink Paella

INGREDIENTS (FOR 4–6)

For the shellfish

1 lb [455 g] cockles or clams

8 oz [230 g] mussels

1 cup [240 ml] white wine

4 garlic cloves, whole

2 tsp red pepper flakes

For the mushroom stock

4 cups [150 g] dried shiitakes

8 cups [2 L] water

For the rice

1 cup [200 g] Arborio rice

2 Tbsp extra-virgin olive oil

1 medium onion, finely chopped

6 garlic cloves, minced

1 tsp smoked paprika

1 tsp salt

To finish

2 tsp squid or cuttlefish ink

2 scallions, finely chopped

2 Tbsp unsalted butter

1 in [2.5 cm] piece ginger, peeled and finely grated

METHOD OF PREPARATION

1. *To prepare the shellfish:* Clean the shellfish under cold water. Scrub off any residue and set aside in separate bowls.

2. *To make the mushroom stock:* In a medium saucepan, cover the mushrooms with the water and bring to a boil over high heat. Lower the heat and simmer for 30 minutes. Strain and reserve the liquid—you should have about 4 cups [1 L] of stock. Reserve 1 cup [250 ml] of the mushrooms, slice into thin pieces, and set aside.

3. While the mushroom stock is simmering, make the rice: Toast the rice in a heavy-bottomed pan over medium heat until fragrant, stirring frequently with a wooden spoon, 4 to 6 minutes. Get a tiny bit of color on it, but nothing too toasty or the grains will dry out. Transfer to a bowl and set aside.

4. *To cook the shellfish:* In a medium pot with a tight-fitting lid, bring wine, garlic, and red pepper flakes to a boil. Once bubbling, drop the cockles in and cover until they begin to open, about 2 minutes. Quickly remove with a slotted spoon and set aside. Repeat with the mussels. Strain the liquid through a fine-mesh strainer to remove any sand or silt and set aside.

5. *To cook the rice:* In the heavy-bottomed pot used to toast the rice, add the olive oil and onion and sauté over medium heat until translucent, about 5 minutes. Add the garlic, smoked paprika, and salt and sauté another 3 minutes or so. Add the rice back to the pot and stir to combine. Add the reserved wine/shellfish liquid, stirring constantly with a wooden spoon until the liquid is absorbed into the rice. Stirring will help release the starches, making the rice creamy and delicious.

6. Add the reserved mushroom stock, 1 cup [250 ml] at a time, to the rice and onion mixture, stirring constantly. Each time the liquid is absorbed into the rice, add another cup of stock and continue stirring. Repeat until at least 3 cups [750 ml] of the stock have been used. Taste the rice, which should be soft and creamy but slightly al dente on the inside. If it needs a bit more liquid, add a little at a time. This whole process will take about 20 minutes.

7. *To finish the rice:* A few minutes before the rice is ready, throw in the squid ink, scallions, butter, and ginger. Stir briskly until the ink has fully incorporated, then place the opened shellfish over the rice. Reduce the heat to the lowest setting and cover. Allow to steam for 2 to 3 minutes.

8. Serve immediately and enjoy, ideally with a glass of tempranillo and a salad of your choice.

Seasoned, Not Sauced by Bowen Yang

ACTOR, COMEDIAN

I am one of those weird people who doesn't like their mapo tofu stewy, or moist, or swimming in sauce. I don't appreciate the colloidal properties of what a generally imagined mapo tofu would be. My mother is, um, only a moderately skilled cook. She wasn't really one for domesticity, but she did her best. I took it out on her a little too often as a child, telling her directly how much I didn't enjoy her cooking, which fills me with a lot of guilt and shame now.

She would always make, and still makes, her mapo tofu extremely dry, which has somehow made me acquire the taste for dry mapo tofu. I like it with a firm tofu, and I like it seasoned and not sauced, though there's still a layer of sauce and obviously the tofu absorbs the peppercorn and the doubanjiang. It absorbs all those flavors and complements the minced pork that tradition calls for. It's very dry and sits perfectly on a bed of white rice. But it's one of the "mistakes" that has made me appreciate my mother's cooking now because it is what I am used to, and I realize that she has been able to pass down this weird anomaly to my palate, which informs what I like eating nowadays.

It's the first thing I ask her to make when I go home to Colorado, where she lives with my dad. It is just about the most comforting food that someone else can make for me. I can only hope that my love for her specific, errant, incorrect kind of mapo tofu makes up for all the years that I was not so gracious and kind about her cooking.

ODDBALL by Michael W. Twitty

AUTHOR, CULINARY HISTORIAN

My mother was making a pot of soup. It had beans in it, and at the time, I didn't like beans. Fifteen beans to be exact, an onion, and a ham bone saved over from the holiday. It matters that I didn't want any and wouldn't eat with her. We had nothing to share. I was just watching her make the soup, with a scowl.

I was tense, but she was tenser. A year before, I had come out at sixteen years old— I don't remember how, but I asserted myself. And every Saturday after that I would go to SMYAL, the Sexual Minority Youth Assistant League, DC's LGBTQ youth group then located in an upstairs loft in Capitol Hill, not far from the Library of Congress. There was nothing drastic about my journey. I mean, I did come out in my school newspaper and I wanted to be seen, but more than that I wanted to be loved for who I had always known myself to be.

She kept stirring. I think the stirring was passive-aggressive, but I don't know that for a fact; we are an often nonverbal culture where gestures are encyclopedias of emotion. My lips wanted to move but they didn't. I kept starting to breathe, then stopping, massaging all the hesitation on my teeth and through my nose. The soup smelled good, but I still didn't want any. I had no hunger, but then I pushed it out:

"There's this community forum in the city next week. I volunteered to speak, can I go?"

"A community forum on what?" My mother stopped stirring.

"On gay rights and gay teens."

"No, I don't think that's a good idea. You can't go."

For the first time in a long time, my mother said I couldn't go anywhere or do something.

"But, Mom, I volunteered and I will be safe riding the Metro—"

"Michael, you are MY child and I said NO!" The wooden spoon almost broke as she tapped it on the edge of the big pot. "Why . . . why do you always have to be the FUCKING ODDBALL of the family?"

"I . . . ummm . . . don't . . . "

I had no answer for her. Oddball? Fucking oddball? This was news to me. I thought until that moment that it was okay to be myself. I didn't know that I was the different one, the odd one, the stranger in our own gates. I was heartbroken and I wanted to die. I've heard those words every single day of my life since.

It wasn't until my mom passed almost twenty years later that I revisited that moment. I really wasn't the oddball of the family; the family was full of oddballs, and that's what made her so mad other than the fact that she was trying to protect me from my own vulnerabilities and was failing miserably. My mother wanted normalcy; she had Black Ozzie and Harriet fantasies, and as time moved on, our family's inherent dysfunction drifted her further and further away from the dream to be, as she once put it, "garden-variety African Americans."

This was the same woman who sat me down and gave me the Van Gogh talk. She explained that his brother Theo tried to encourage Vincent out of his depression by exhorting him to value and invest in his happiness and self-esteem. She read me his letters. I had to make myself happy and find joy in my truth. But I was her oddball.

Unless it meant being gay. Mom didn't mean the harm she caused and I never brought it up. One day she said randomly, "I'm sorry for anything I've said or done that hurt you." It hurt too much to unbury the words, but my mother's love was unquestioned—faults and all. And yet, I'm pretty sure if I ever got a tattoo—and I won't—it would say "oddball."

Without a Gathering, a Good Salad
by Alice Waters

AUTHOR, CHEF, FOOD ACTIVIST

I'm sure many people feel this way, but I can say with certainty that I've never lived through any period more professionally and personally challenging than the pandemic. I've witnessed many passages of cultural upheaval: the Vietnam War, Women's Liberation, the Civil Rights Movement, the AIDS crisis (to name just a handful). But there's something about this time that I've found to be especially devastating. I opened my restaurant, Chez Panisse, in 1971 with a bunch of close friends. We wanted it to be a place where people could gather and eat together; a place for the community, but also a refuge for activists, fomenters, and anyone who had been marginalized by mainstream American society. We were Berkeley hippies who had radical ideas about how we wanted to live, talk, create, love, and share. At its core, Chez Panisse was built on these mutually held values. At the beginning of the pandemic, I was reminded of the early days of AIDS, when no one really understood what we were facing—not scientifically, but not culturally either. AIDS patients became pariahs. People I knew and loved were getting sick, and few places felt safe from persecution and scrutiny. I was determined to keep the restaurant open to all, for it to be a haven, even as many were being overcome by fear.

Back in February of 2020, I thought coronavirus might be similar. We've been open for nearly fifty years—we've seen disasters, overcome obstacles. I imagined Chez Panisse might once again be the gathering place it has been during periods of turmoil. But, of course, we quickly learned that gathering was in fact precisely what we should not do. We decided to close the restaurant. It was one of the hardest moments of my life.

I live by myself and am completely dependent on the restaurant for my social world. It's not just a place to bring my friends to dinner, or feed the people I love; the restaurant itself is my companion. And I wasn't just worried about myself, of course; I was worried about the more than one hundred employees who make up what I call "La Famille Panisse." How could I continue to take care of them? How could I take care of the farmers who depended on us for their survival? We very quickly figured out how to offer our customers the pristine produce we once

prepared for them directly in the form of farm boxes, and then slowly built up to a take-out business. Through all of this change, the agony of uncertainty, and the real, genuine loneliness of this time, I've looked forward to the beautiful boxes of salad greens delivered to me from the restaurant. Each day, opening my box of perfect greens from my friend Bob Cannard and his son Ross's farm—sometimes blushing pink chicories like rose petals, with slices of grapefruit. Sometimes spicy arugula with salty toasted hazelnuts and ricotta salata. A good salad will buoy my spirits. A good salad—I now realize—will help see me through calamity.

This is a recipe for our classic Chez Panisse vinaigrette. It is the sauce I make most often, and if it's made out of good olive oil and good wine vinegar, it's the best salad dressing I can imagine. At its simplest, vinaigrette is a mixture of vinegar and oil in a ratio of one part vinegar to about three or four parts oil. Start by estimating roughly how much vinaigrette you will need. This depends on what you're using it for; a quarter cup is more than enough for four servings of green salad, for example, but you really never need to measure out exact amounts. Start by pouring the vinegar into a bowl. Dissolve a pinch of salt in it and taste for balance. The salt has a real relationship with the vinegar. When you add just enough salt, it subdues the acid of the vinegar and brings it into a wonderful balance. Try adding salt bit by bit and tasting to see what happens. How much salt is too much? How much is too little? What tastes best? If you add too much salt, just add a touch more vinegar.

Grind in some black pepper and whisk in the oil. The vinaigrette should taste brightly balanced, neither too oily nor overly acidic. Adjust the sauce, adding more vinegar if you've added too much oil, and more salt, if it needs it.

Classic Chez Panisse Vinaigrette

1 Tbsp red wine vinegar

Salt and freshly ground black pepper

3 to 4 Tbsp [45 to 60 ml] extra-virgin olive oil

METHOD OF PREPARATION

1. Pour the red wine vinegar into a small bowl.

2. Add salt and black pepper. Stir to dissolve the salt. Adjust to taste.

3. With a fork or a small whisk, beat in the extra-virgin olive oil a little at a time.

4. Taste as you go and stop when it tastes right.

VARIATIONS

- Add a little puréed garlic or diced shallot, or both, to the vinegar.

- White wine vinegar, sherry vinegar, or lemon juice can replace some or all of the red wine vinegar.

- Beat in a little mustard before you start adding the oil.

- For part of the olive oil, substitute a very fresh nut oil, such as walnut or hazelnut.

- Heavy cream or crème fraîche can replace some or all of the olive oil.

- Chop some fresh herbs and stir them into the finished vinaigrette.

The Best of the Worst by Laurie Woolever

WRITER, EDITOR

A few years ago, in late spring, my unhappy marriage imploded, messily and inevitably, one terrible Monday night. It was both a massive relief and a terrifying tectonic shift. I started sleeping on the couch. The next morning, I made an emergency call to my longtime therapist, but she couldn't really talk for long, she said, because her husband had just died unexpectedly, violently, and the police were still in her home. I turned to the nonprofessional advice of others.

My boss, Tony Bourdain, who was a mentor to me and many others, a generous, charismatic, mysterious, and brilliant person around whom many universes were centered, was reassuring when I told him that I was getting divorced and looking for a new home. He'd been through it, too.

"It's gonna suck, a lot, at first," he said. "But then you're gonna realize how much better off you are. Don't get a shitty apartment because you think you can't afford something better," he said. "Whatever you need, I will help you." I got myself a good apartment, secure in the knowledge that he would have my back.

A month later, he took his own life.

I was subsisting on Hi-Chew candy and nicotine gum, too unmoored and anxious to eat normally. On the day that the news of Tony's death broke, a cruelly bright and perfect summer Friday, my friend Alison invited me into her cool, shaded kitchen, handed me a can of seltzer, and made me a bowl of soft scrambled eggs, the best thing I'd eaten, or would eat, that summer.

Soft Scrambled Eggs

INGREDIENTS (FOR 2)

4 eggs

2 Tbsp butter

Salt and pepper

METHOD OF PREPARATION

1. Crack the eggs into a bowl and gently whip them with a fork to break the yolks and mostly incorporate the yolks and whites. If you really want soft and creamy scrambled eggs, you shouldn't go crazy here; whisking vigorously incorporates more air, which makes for firmer, drier scrambled eggs.

2. In a medium skillet, preferably nonstick, heat the butter over medium heat until it forms tiny foamy bubbles that then subside.

3. Reduce the heat to medium-low, pour the eggs into the pan, and swirl them around a bit. Use a wooden spoon or rubber or silicone spatula to gently and more or less continuously move the eggs around as they cook, in a loose figure-eight pattern, making sure to hit all parts of the pan, releasing steam and keeping the eggs from cooking too quickly.

4. As soon as the eggs are cooked through but still soft, which should only take a few minutes, remove the pan from the heat, season the eggs with as much salt and pepper as you like, divide them between two shallow bowls, and serve immediately, with buttered toast or whatever else appeals.

It's gonna suck,
a lot, at first.
But then you're
gonna realize
how much better
off you are.

Portrait of a Single Father by Cey Adams

ARTIST

My only son, Eric, was born in the winter of 1984. I remember thinking I was not prepared to be a twenty-year-old dad. I was completely scared and unsure that I had any real-life parenting skills. My older sister, sensing I was looking for moral support, sat me down at the kitchen table with a bowl of our mom's warm bread pudding, and reminded me of my responsibilities as his father. After I finished eating and listening, I felt calm enough to make some decisions about my future. I decided to put my teenage graffiti-writing shenanigans behind me and become a man. I grabbed a piece of paper, made a list of business contacts and anyone I felt could help move my art career forward, and officially set up shop as a professional artist and graphic designer. I did anything—from gallery exhibitions, murals, and commissioned pieces to logo designs and advertising campaigns for corporate brands. I quickly learned that being an independent, small business owner meant doing everything on my own. Up to this point, the difficulties working parents faced from day to day had never occurred to me. But as a single father in New York City, bringing my son to work sites and meetings became a normal routine.

In the early 1980s, it was beyond uncommon to see a young dad like myself changing a dirty diaper in a public space. I remember one time we were headed to DC by train to visit family. As we sat in the lounge area waiting to board, I suddenly smelled something sour coming from my baby's onesie. I knew this was going to get messy real quick! Imagine me running around Penn Station, two bags over my shoulder, holding my son and looking for a restroom. Looking back, it felt like a scene in a movie. There I was running around the city holding a bomb that was about to explode!

I located the nearest restroom and dashed inside. Not only was there no changing station or table, but the place was filthy and smelly. The floor was a wet, slippery combination of footprints, mud, and urine from guys peeing anywhere and everywhere. Yuck!! I looked down at my little boy's sweet face and knew what I had to do. Without hesitation, I took off my jacket, laid it down on the nasty floor, and changed his dirty diaper. I felt a strange joy come over me. I was proud to be a father!

Once we were comfortable and settled on the train, I thought: Everything is going to be okay. I thought about my life and my son's life. I imagined the aroma of my mom's warm bread pudding again . . . Calm set in. Eric closed his eyes, I closed mine, and we both drifted off to sleep.

Bread Pudding

INGREDIENTS (FOR 4)

For the bread pudding

1 cup [140 ml] raisins

¼ cup [60 ml] Kentucky bourbon

1 loaf French bread, at least a day old

4 cups [960 ml] milk

3 large eggs

2 cups [400 g] sugar

2 Tbsp vanilla extract

¼ tsp allspice

½ tsp ground cinnamon

3 Tbsp butter, melted

For the bourbon sauce

½ cup [110 g] butter

1 cup [200 g] sugar

1 large egg

½ cup [120 ml] Kentucky bourbon [less or more to taste]

METHOD OF PREPARATION

1. *To make the bread pudding:* In a small bowl, combine the raisins and bourbon. Cover and soak for 1 to 2 hours.

2. Preheat the oven to 350°F (180°C).

3. Cut the bread into 1 in [2.5 cm] cubes.

4. Place the milk in a large mixing bowl and add the bread. Press the bread into the milk until all milk is absorbed.

5. In a separate bowl, whisk the eggs, then add the sugar, vanilla, allspice, and cinnamon and whisk together. Pour over the bread and milk mixture.

6. Add the bourbon-soaked raisins (with or without the remaining soaking liquid, according to taste). Stir gently to combine.

7. Pour the melted butter into the bottom of a 9 by 13 in [23 by 33 cm] baking pan, coating the bottom and sides. Pour the bread, milk, and egg mixture into the baking pan.

8. Bake for 35 to 45 minutes, until the liquid is set. The pudding is done when the edges brown and pull away from the sides of the pan. This can also be made in individual ramekins.

9. *While the bread pudding is baking, make the sauce:* Melt the butter in a medium saucepan over low heat. Add the sugar and egg and whisk to blend well.

10. Slowly cook over low heat, stirring constantly, until the mixture thickens enough to coat the back of a spoon, then remove from the heat. Do not allow the mixture to simmer, or the sauce will curdle. If the sauce curdles, take it off the heat and blend it smooth in a blender.

11. Whisk in the bourbon to taste. Whisk again before serving. The sauce should be soft, creamy, and smooth.

12. Serve the bread pudding with the bourbon sauce on the side.

Pesto to Pass Time by Chelsea Peretti

ACTOR, WRITER, COMEDIAN

Chelsea Peretti: You know what I made a ton of in the pandemic is pesto. Pesto with tons of garlic, and then I put lemon zest in it. I put it in my mini Cuisinart, and everything about it is so zippy.

Alison Riley: Right, it's refreshing.

CP: It's like also kind of a depression food cause it cuts through—the basil, the garlic, the lemon—and if you don't respond to one of those with some part of your body, then you are in a truly dark place.

AR: Do you make it and freeze it or do you just make it per meal?

CP: No, my mom is all about freezing things all the time... She's like, "Actually, you can put it in ice cube trays..." but I don't like defrosting. I feel like defrosting is a whole science. What's appealing about pesto is the freshness of it and the vitality of it, and it's so easy to make. I don't feel the need to freeze for the future.

AR: And cooking passes pandemic time.

CP: Yes, it was a good pandemic malaise recipe because part of the pandemic was living out the same day over and over and trying to find ways to keep yourself stimulated and excited to be alive. Turns out, that's pesto.

Basil Pesto

Disclaimer: Italian traditionalists, please be aware this is some California-style improvisation. Please don't be mad at me!

INGREDIENTS (FOR 2)

1 cup [240 ml] extra-virgin olive oil

1 lemon

½ cup [60 g] pine nuts

¾ cup [25 g] grated Parmesan

2 cups [25 g] basil leaves

1 to 3 garlic cloves, peeled

Salt

METHOD OF PREPARATION

1. Fill the bottom of a mini food processor with olive oil to about ½ in [1.3 cm] high.

2. Slice or zest (yellow skin only) half of a lemon and add that to the food processor.

3. In a small skillet, brown the pine nuts, adding a handful or more to taste (or budget). I'm sure some other nut could work in a pinch. Add them to the food processor.

4. Add the Parmesan.

5. Add two handfuls of basil leaves (I include buds but remove stems).

6. Add the garlic depending on how depressed you are.

7. Add salt (or truffle salt!) to taste.

8. Blend until a paste forms. Add more olive oil to loosen. Taste and add more of anything that is missing.

If you don't respond to one of those with some part of your body, then you are in a truly dark place.

A Balm Then, a Balm Now by Tien Nguyen
WRITER

When I was about thirteen, my mother started working two, three jobs a week, pulling a double or triple most days. This meant she usually left very early and returned home very late. My sisters and I made do with microwavable dinners, Kraft Mac and Cheese, sandwiches. Sometimes, though, my mom got home early enough and rustled up what she named trứng flat ("flat eggs"): eggs beaten with fish sauce, pepper, and chopped scallions, cooked like a giant omelet, and eaten with steamed rice. It took all of five minutes to throw together. Combining fish sauce with eggs is so common in Vietnamese households that I'm sure others grew up eating some version of this, too. Still, for us, trứng flat was a real treat and fed us through some miserable times.

Not too long ago, I learned of a homey northern Vietnamese dish called chả trứng chiên. Most variations involve beating eggs with fish sauce, pepper, and scallions before adding seasoned ground chicken or pork to the mix. If you're flush, crab or mussels aren't out of place, either. The point is, meat is a very common ingredient—and that meat is the difference between a trứng flat and a chả trứng chiên. I've realized, belatedly, that had she not been short on two things (time, money), my mom might have made chả trứng chiên instead of trứng flat. It's hard for me not to think of trứng flat now as a dish of both survival and omission. Still, I have a right fondness for it. I make it when I'm blue, or when I need a quick meal. It was a balm then. It is a balm now.

It's hard for me
not to think of
trứng flat now
as a dish of
both survival
and omission.

Trứng Flat (Flat Eggs)

I use an 8 in [20 cm] nonstick pan for this, but you can use any pan you have on hand, though a larger pan will result in a flatter trứng flat (as the eggs will spread more), and, conversely, a smaller pan will yield a thicker one. This recipe can easily be scaled up as needed, and leftovers can be transferred to an airtight container and refrigerated for up to 3 days.

INGREDIENTS (FOR 2)

3 large eggs

2 to 3 scallions, white and green parts, sliced, plus more for serving

1 tsp fish sauce, plus more for serving

Freshly ground black pepper

1 Tbsp unsalted butter

Steamed rice, for serving

Furikake, for serving

METHOD OF PREPARATION

1. Crack the eggs into a large bowl and add the scallions, fish sauce, and a pinch of black pepper. Beat well to combine.

2. In an 8 in [20 cm] pan set over medium-low heat, melt the butter. When it begins to froth, pour in the eggs. Cook, undisturbed, until the eggs are set, just a few minutes. Then, using a spatula, divide the eggs in half. Carefully flip each half over and cook until that side has set, 30 seconds to 1 minute. Slide the eggs onto a serving plate and cut into squares or wedges.

3. To serve, scoop steamed rice into a bowl. Place the trứng flat on top and garnish with chopped scallions. Taste. If you think it needs a little extra oomph, drizzle the bowl with fish sauce or a sprinkle of furikake. Enjoy.

Forget All Your Troubles
by Joan As Police Woman

COMPOSER, SINGER, MULTI-INSTRUMENTALIST

I don't associate food with a specific event. I associate food with every event. The best, all-purpose food that comes to mind is a simple Japanese sweet potato drowned in coconut manna or coconut oil or, best of all, both. It combines sweet, savory, and fatty in ideal degrees. After more than ten years of eating them often, I've yet to get tired of them. Also, they fill you up, unlike chocolate, which just makes you want more chocolate.

I make them whether I am sad or not. But sadness at any level, all of the sadness, is just eradicated by these beauties. They turn sunshiny yellow in the middle and have gorgeous purply pink skin. They're nutty, they're sweet, they're perfect. These sweet potatoes have a built-in olfactory alarm that alerts you when they're almost done—you start to wonder who's baking cookies and then realize it's coming from your own oven. If you do it right, they also have texture, and the skin gets crispy. You are required to eat the skin. Don't even fuck around with not eating the skin. You can't come to my house and not eat the skin.

Roasted Japanese Sweet Potato

INGREDIENTS (FOR 1)

1 Japanese sweet potato

Coconut butter or oil

Salt and pepper

METHOD OF PREPARATION

1. Preheat the oven to 425°F [220°C]. Line a baking dish with parchment paper or foil.

2. With gusto, lovingly stab the Japanese sweet potato with a long, thin blade, remembering you need to preserve the hand that's holding the potato.

3. Roast uncovered for 50 minutes to 1½ hours depending on the size. While roasting, natural caramelization may begin seeping out the holes in the skin—do not fret, simply rejoice. It is ready when it is easily squishable and when the knife slides through the middle with no problem.

4. Slice the potato open and slather on the coconut butter/oil and close it up again so it melts. Season with salt and pepper as desired. Again, the skin is the best part, so don't dare try to discard it.

5. Forget all your troubles.

Sadness at any level, all of the sadness, is just eradicated by these beauties.

A Mess for a Moment by Hassan Pierre

SUSTAINABLE FASHION PIONEER

Alison Riley: Have you ever had a broken heart?

Hassan Pierre: Luckily, no. In the last ten years I have had two serious partners, but I have broken up with both of them.

AR: When you break up with somebody, do you let loose or do you take a little time, or is there no rule?

HP: I have maintained friendships with both of my exes and they're still two of my really good friends. Even though I was breaking up with them—maybe it was a little bit of a heartbreak—there was nothing done in either direction with a malicious intent that would require me to feel like breaking loose or in need of a big release. I am out all the time anyway, no matter what.

AR: Is there any one food you crave when you are feeling sad?

HP: This sounds ridiculous, but peanut butter with melted chocolate and coconut flakes.

AR: That does not sound ridiculous, that sounds delicious.

HP: Anytime I'm sad, that is my go-to comfort food. I melt my own chocolate chips in a double boiler, and then I add some peanut butter, add some coconut flakes, and then I take a banana and dip the banana in there.

AR: Is this the kind of thing you eat over the stove?

HP: Yes. I eat it right over the stove, with a spoon, chocolate gets everywhere, coconut flakes, peanut butter, the whole thing.

It's a one-stop shop and you're done. All better.

AR: *When was the last time you had this?*

HP: Two weeks ago, maybe? I was really missing my significant other a lot, so I decided to eat some of my banana chocolate mess.

AR: *That sounds like it would definitely make you feel better.*

HP: It hits the spot EVERY time.

AR: *Have you ever made that for anybody else?*

HP: No—it is not something I have told anyone either.

AR: *Has anyone seen you eat it?*

HP: One friend on FaceTime has caught glimpses.

AR: *And do you make a portion you can kill in one sitting?*

HP: Yes, I have it down to a science. One banana, I know the amount of chocolate chips and the peanut butter I like, and the coconut flakes. It's a one-stop shop and you're done. All better.

Coasting in on an Empty Tank
by Nicholas Galanin

ARTIST, MUSICIAN

Spring was here, I had just finished community college and planned on driving north, back to Alaska, with my few belongings and my younger brother. It was our first solo road trip together, and we had a map to get us to Canada. This was B.C.—before cell phones—so the copilot map-reading job was important.

We set off, and after several long stretches on the road, my brother and I learned a few things: One, that my prized CD collection had become the most important necessity, a curated collection of punk rock classics, and two, that my budgeting skills were on the optimistic side. We stopped in Seattle to see old family friends before crossing the border, and luckily their mother lovingly snuck an extra sixty dollars into our pockets as we said goodbye.

Right on schedule, we drove toward a small coastal community, set to arrive on the day the ferry would depart for Alaska. On the way, we (I) miscalculated the distance from one gas station to the next and realized we were not only in danger of missing the boat, but it was also likely that we wouldn't even make it to the next pump. The solution was to coast whenever possible and to press the gas pedal only when necessary. The car literally died when we hit the next gas station— we coasted in on an empty tank.

Filling up this thirsty vehicle and feeling relief, I went in to pay . . . declined . . . declined . . . declined. The service station clerk knew I had no other options and kindly offered to rifle through my CD collection as payment for the gas. With no other option, I allowed the unthinkable. All of my favorite albums and compilations became hers. While her greasy gas station mitts continued selecting gem after gem in the form of compact disc, I looked away. I spotted an ancient ATM in the corner of the store. I stuck my card in, knowing that my bank account was at zero. But for some reason the machine spit out a Canadian $20 bill. Amazing. With a three-day boat ride ahead, I had to let her keep the CDs and save the twenty for food. We made it to the boat. We didn't eat well but we ate, and we rationed these meals to get the most bang for our Canadian buck:

Alaska marine highway hot dogs, dry from rolling on the hot dog spinning machine overnight, Jell-O fruit cups full of canned fruit, and, of course, free water with crushed ice. The hot dogs stretched far with free condiments, and the crushed ice was something to chew on.

Fruit Gelatin Cups

INGREDIENTS (FOR 4)

1 cup [240 ml] apple juice

1 cup [240 ml] cranberry juice

One 3 oz [85 g] packet unflavored gelatin

2 cups [280 g] fruit cut into bite-size pieces [apples, berries, pineapple, cherries, peaches, or bananas]

1 tsp lemon juice

METHOD OF PREPARATION

1. Mix the juices together in a mixing bowl. Pour ¼ cup [60 ml] into a small saucepan on the stove. Sprinkle the gelatin over the surface of the juice in the pan. Avoid getting any on the sides, as it could burn.

2. Divide the fruit among four 4 oz [120 g] ramekins, and give them a light tap to settle the pieces into the cups.

3. Bring the juice to a boil while whisking. Boil for 1 minute, then pour back into the reserved juice. Add the lemon juice and stir to cool slightly.

4. Pour the juice mixture over the fruit, dividing it evenly.

5. Place in the refrigerator for 1 to 2 hours, or until the gelatin is set.

To Accompany Pig by Bob Power

RECORD PRODUCER, ENGINEER, MIXER

On the eve of the 2016 election, in excited anticipation of our first woman president, I made a reservation at a wonderful rustic-yet-high-end Italian joint by Gramercy Park in Manhattan.

I asked for one of the few booths along one wall—easier to talk there amid the lively, buzzing atmosphere. In my mind, I imagined all the engaged folks at the other tables as virtuous lefties happily anticipating, as I, a positive social agenda for the next four years.

We were seated around 8 p.m., still too early for any substantive exit polls. While the campaign polls had not been overwhelming, I think I harbored a deep-seated belief that no one as dim and transparent as Trump could actually be elected president. Inside, I felt that it would be akin to someone like Bozo the Clown—or at least Silvio Berlusconi—inhabiting the White House.

When our table was ready, we brought our half-finished martinis from the bar where we had been waiting. And although normally I feel it's degrading to a fine dining experience, we had no compunction about checking our phones every ten or fifteen minutes for any news.

The meal started well enough with a beautifully seared polpo appetizer. These folks have a way with heat—both slow and fast. For the main, I splurged (hey, it's Hillary!) and went for the house specialty: maialino al forno, an exquisitely slow-roasted pig, with oh-so-crispy skin (removed and cooked separately, then replaced on the pig, I believe, for optimum crisping) accompanied by an Etna Rosso.

As more definitive news began to drift in over the course of this wondrous meal, any initial (or later, alcohol-fueled) positive anticipation began to be overtaken by a depressing cloud of doubt, colored in a dull gray-brown, more of a creeping depression than a sudden jolt of bad news; a slow leak from a toilet that, at first, you want to ignore, until the thin layer of brown water is clearly making a statement, slowly spreading over the bathroom floor.

A slow leak from a toilet that, at first, you want to ignore.

By the time we were two-thirds through the main, it was pretty clear that things were not going our way. What a dichotomy . . . making our way through this marvelous meal, revealing more delights with every bite and sip, while the other, political, spiritual, and moral side of the scale was dipping in perfect coordination with the rising gustatory end.

Bob's Roasted Cauliflower Side Dish

INGREDIENTS
(FOR 2 AS A MAIN,
FOR 4 AS A SIDE)

1 large cauliflower

2 Tbsp good-quality olive oil

1 large lemon, juiced, rinds reserved

Sea salt

Pinch of cayenne powder [not for heat, just to wake up the flavors]

4 tsp dried oregano

2 bay leaves

1 tsp chopped fresh thyme

1 tsp chopped fresh rosemary

2 Tbsp pine nuts

2 Tbsp chopped kalamata olives

Freshly ground black pepper

METHOD OF PREPARATION

1. Preheat the oven to 375°F (190°C). Line a baking sheet with foil.

2. Wash and break up the cauliflower by hand into bite-size pieces. You can include thicker stems if desired—they are underappreciated. Place in a large mixing bowl. Add the olive oil and lemon juice. Toss. Chop the lemon rind into ½ in [1.3 cm] pieces and add to the bowl.

3. Add the salt, cayenne, oregano, bay leaves, thyme, and rosemary, pinching the fresh herbs to release their flavor. Toss to coat the cauliflower in the seasonings.

4. Spread out the cauliflower on the prepared baking sheet. Less crowding = better browning. Roast for 25 to 30 minutes, until the cauliflower pieces are browned with some blackened spots. If you're lucky, the lemon rind will be a bit blackened. If the cauliflower is very dry looking, drizzle with a bit more oil and/or lemon juice.

5. When the cauliflower has browned, sprinkle with the pine nuts. Continue to roast until the nuts are toasted, 3 to 5 more minutes.

6. Remove the baking sheet from the oven and return the cauliflower and nuts to the bowl. Add the chopped olives and a pinch of freshly ground black pepper. Toss.

7. Let sit for 15 to 20 minutes to allow the flavors to meld. Good warm or at room temperature. Goes well with a fruity medium-bodied Italian red or Beaujolais. Or anything.

The Art of Giving by Money Mark

MUSIC NERD

I grew up in the West Athens borough of Los Angeles, which is South Central proper. And after these fifty-plus years of living in SoCal, it is geographically where my heart still resides.

Vandana Shiva remarks that nature's currency is life, and I tasted life every morning while I walked to school—in the alley between Ainsworth Street and Vermont Avenue, crossing 120th Street, downhill to the gates of West Athens Elementary public school. The first two blocks of this quarter-mile trek were an urban orchard. Let me simply name the fruit trees that were my early morning givers: grapefruit, lemon, kumquat, peach, avocado, pomegranate, apricot, guava, and Santa Rosa plums—those were my favorite! These trees are fewer now, but you can still find them in many parts of LA's southern neighborhoods. Funny. Over the decades the so-called affluent neighborhoods have lost their natural botany to "development," but nature offered unconditionally to a young soul as mine, late for class. I received sustenance for half of the day and a life lesson beyond what was written in books: the art of giving.

My mother did make breakfast for us (I'm the middle son of three boys). Maybe fried eggs over Japanese white rice with refried pinto beans. Or fermented pickles and kimchi. Or cheese quesadillas with handmade corn tortillas. You see, my father was Japanese-American from Hawaiʻi, and my mother a straight-up Tejana from San Antonio's Southside—though both their birth certificates claim they are "white." My father's chosen first name was Frank. Jitsuro was his Japanese name. My mother was named after the iconic singer-songwriter activist Lydia Mendoza. Yes, I was eating Japanese burritos in the '70s.

Interracial marriage was illegal in Texas, where they were living, so they migrated north to Michigan to start a family. I was born in Detroit, where my mother first heard about powdered milk and other "modern" processed foods. Detroit had pizza and Greek food and Italian food, but eventually my parents set their sights on Los Angeles and a community that opened its arms to them—where they could readily get Asian food products, Mexican spices, and where I could bite into a juicy peach on my way to school. Oh, damn! I forgot my homework!

Guacamole with Pomegranate and Cotijo Cheese

½ small yellow onion, minced or finely diced

1 tsp minced garlic

1 jalapeño, seeded and minced

2 large or 3 medium ripe avocados, pitted and flesh scooped out

¼ cup [60 ml] fresh lime juice

1 Tbsp kosher salt

½ cup [20 g] chopped cilantro leaves and stems

½ cup [75 g] pomegranate arils

½ cup [60 g] crumbled cotija cheese

METHOD OF PREPARATION

1. In a large mixing bowl, combine the onion, garlic, jalapeño, and avocados. Add the lime juice and salt. Mash and mix gently with a fork, making sure the salt and juice are distributed thoroughly. Taste, and add more salt and/or lime juice as desired.

2. Fold in the cilantro.

3. Transfer to a serving bowl. Garnish with the pomegranate arils and then the cheese. Serve with chips and enjoy!

A life lesson beyond what was written in books: the art of giving.

How to Treat Yourself by Kia Cooks

CHEF, FOUNDER OF KFTP

The lowest point of my life since moving to New York was the summer I left the restaurant Lalito. I think it was actually another chapter of a breakdown in progress, but I had zero mentorship—it wasn't like I was surrounded by elders or other female chefs who might have helped me out and guided me; I was swimming out there on my own, or drowning, before and after I left. Once I was gone, I felt like I'd lost my purpose; I had this whole trajectory planned out for myself that had disappeared. I didn't know what to do with myself.

I didn't want to cook. I realized I couldn't remember how to cook for myself at home. I had spent all my time cooking for fifty to a hundred people every morning and every night and ordering in large quantities. I felt like I didn't know how to shop; I didn't know how to do anything anymore. I was depressed and I was broke. My whole world was asking, *What's next, what's next, what's next?* I was like, "I have only been in New York a short time and this whole thing has been my entire life in a very public way. I don't know what I am doing next, I don't know how to pay my rent. I don't know."

I was struggling for a long time, gliding on this defense mechanism or this protective kind of measure, telling myself this was okay, the universe does things for reasons, blah blah blah. I was trying to contain myself with surface-level affirmations so that I would not burst apart at the seams, only to realize I was trying to prevent a breakdown that I was already in the middle of having. I was lost, for sure.

Then, on August 12, 2019, the Popeyes chicken sandwich dropped. At the time, I lived right around the corner from a Popeyes. It was super cheap but I had no money, and one day I just decided, screw it, I am going to treat myself to that sandwich and see what it's all about. The first thing that blew me away was not the sandwich but the act of getting the sandwich, since I am not used to even having the time to get up and do something, to decide on a whim that I am going to have or do this. That's just not the kind of time I've had before. That felt pretty exhilarating.

And then eating the sandwich—that was the best thing I ever tasted in my life. I had not experienced joy around food in so long before I ate that Popeyes chicken freaking sandwich. I felt like a food critic, tapped in all of a sudden, all about the briny pickle and the batter and the brioche bun. I felt like I knew what I was talking about again because I could engage with food and pleasure and excitement over this fast-food chicken sandwich. It made me feel like a person.

After that, I ate a lot of those chicken sandwiches because it became the thing I would do to treat myself. Before, I'd go have dinner at a friend's restaurant in the city, or buy some wine, or, after a long week when everything went well and no one forgot to order anything, I'd get my check and go get a pair of sneakers on Broadway. I couldn't do that anymore. If anything, I was just celebrating being alive. I was grateful for waking up and sitting down and figuring out how to make money. Once a week, I could get up, get that Popeyes chicken sandwich, and figure out what I was going to do with my life.

I was trying
to prevent
a breakdown
that I was
already in
the middle
of having.

A *Ritual of Hope* by Simon Doonan

AUTHOR, AESTHETE, RABID SOCCER FAN

In the early '80s, on a hot, dry afternoon, I drove my friend Mundo to the doctor to get the result of a biopsy. A weird purple lump had appeared on his neck. It's probably just an ingrown hair.

The doctor was blunt: *This is Kaposi's sarcoma. You have AIDS.*

Can you give my friend a referral to a specialist?

There are no referrals. There are no specialists. This disease is fatal. Are you fellas religious?

We were not religious. We were young and feral and creative and fun-loving. The epic horror of this diagnosis hit us like a ton of shit.

The following day, on the notice board of the Erewhon health food store, I spotted a postcard advertising the Michio Kushi macrobiotic center in West Hollywood. Listed among the conditions that the macrobiotic diet might alleviate was—drumroll!—AIDS.

Mundo went to the center and had a cooking lesson, and then I joined him. We learned about the macro philosophy of George Ozawa. One day, Michio Kushi, the macro guru-in-chief, came to the center and gave Mundo a one-on-one consultation, after which he lit up a cigarette. Mundo was very amused by this.

Mundo died a few months later.

In the 1990s, I read an article that stated that the macro diet is far too radical for AIDS patients, especially people who make extreme changes from, for example, lardy Mexican food (me and Mundo) to ascetic Japanese fare.

Oh fuck!

After cutting out animal protein, Mundo had lost a dramatic amount of weight—
I could have a modeling career!—and his lesions proliferated rapidly. I remember
sitting in a movie with Mundo and his boyfriend Jef. He showed us a couple
of sarcomas that had erupted on his wrist *during the movie.*

For a while I cringed with regret over Mundo's macro interlude. But the truth of
the matter is that Mundo was not long for this world, and macrobiotics was the only
thing that offered him any kind of hope. The process of preparing his miso soup
was a ritual of hope, a simple task that gave him a life-affirming moment in his day.

Macro Miso Soup

INGREDIENTS (FOR 2)

2 Tbsp wakame, soaked in
water for 2 to 3 minutes to
soften, drained, and cut into
strips*

2 cups [480 ml] spring water

*2 Tbsp thinly sliced carrot,
daikon, turnip, or squash*

2 Tbsp miso paste

*½ cup [10 g] finely chopped
kale, chard, or spinach*

1 Tbsp sliced scallion

**Wakame is a dried seaweed
found in many specialty
groceries or health food
stores. The soup is best made
utilizing its unique flavor,
though in a pinch, you could
use a couple pieces of
nori. In that case, add the
nori with your greens.*

METHOD OF PREPARATION

1. In a pot, combine the soaked wakame and spring water.
   Bring to a boil.

2. Add the carrot, lower the heat, and let the broth come to
   a simmer.

3. Place the miso in a small mixing bowl and, using a ladle,
   add a small amount of broth while stirring to dissolve
   the miso paste so it easily mingles with the rest of the soup.
   Add the miso and kale to the broth and stir to combine.

4. Lower the heat and allow the soup to simmer slowly for
   2 to 3 minutes.

5. Serve in a warmed bowl, garnished with the scallion.

The thing about
a pot of beans
is that it can
feed a bunch of
people at once,
in good times
and in bad.

Beans for All Time by Liz Lambert

HOTELIER, DESIGNER

Pinto beans. A heavy-bottomed pot of beans, simmering on the stove in a crowded kitchen, murmurs and laughter, glasses clinking. In a lonely kitchen, a meditation.

Pinto beans were one of the first things I learned to cook when I was young, watching Viola, our longtime caregiver, at the stove. I feel like I have made them a thousand times since then. I made them out at the ranch after my mother's funeral, made them dozens of times for the stragglers staying over after a music festival, made them when the pantry was bare and there was no other way to feed my friends.

Beans were the center of a casual family dinner on Sundays in Austin with my brother, Lou, for years. We would make a crock of brown rice, pick up a roast chicken and some fresh tortillas, and set out bowls of shredded cabbage, slices of radish, chopped cucumbers with salt and vinegar, cut avocado, salsa, and escabeche (and Mrs. Renfro's Chow Chow, if you could find it). But the main event was always the beans.

The thing about a pot of beans is that it can feed a bunch of people at once, in good times and in bad. You can make several meals from one pot, and smash some up to serve on burritos later. You can make them vegetarian, just salt and simmering water, or add a ham hock for a deep umami flavor. Chicken stock is a nice way to flavor the pot. Beans are easy to make once you settle on your preferred method.

Age-old wisdom is that beans must be presoaked overnight, or quick soaked by bringing the pot to a boil, covering with a lid, shutting off the heat, and letting it sit for an hour. There is a current school of thought, however, that you don't need to soak the beans, just begin cooking in cold water. This method will increase your cooking time, but some folks swear it increases flavor. Use a heavy-bottomed pot, with enough liquid to cover the beans by 2 in [5 cm]. Bring to a boil for 5 to 10 minutes, then lower the heat to a simmer.

Once you've got the beans soaked or not soaked and at a simmer, add a rough-chopped onion, a few heads of crushed garlic, a few tsp of chili powder, and salt to taste, and cook for 3 to 4 hours, adding liquid as needed. Add a can of crushed tomatoes, if you've got one, after the beans have softened—highly acidic ingredients like tomatoes will slow the cooking time and toughen the skins, which is maddening, trust me. The beans will be ready when the broth is milky and the beans are tender, and some of the beans have begun to come apart. I like to add a tsp of brown sugar or maple syrup near the end of the cooking.

TO SERVE WITH YOUR BEANS

Pot of brown rice

Chopped cucumbers, set aside with salt and vinegar

Shredded cabbage, also salted, with a spike of vinegar

Chow chow, or pickled things in general

Thin slivers of radish

Sliced avocado

Salsa, escabeche, or jalapeños

Roasted chicken

Stack of good tortillas

Put everything in one bowl, beginning with a bed of brown rice, then the beans, and finish with your choice of the above (chicken and tortillas to the side).

She would fry those potatoes within an inch of their life.

Crispy, Hot, Salty Potatoes by Justin Vivian Bond

CABARET ENCHANTRESS, ACTOR, VISUAL ARTIST

My mom didn't really like cooking too much. But one thing she did love making was crispy fried potatoes. She'd thinly slice potatoes, slice some onion, heat up a skillet with oil or butter, and she would fry those potatoes within an inch of their life: crispy, hot, salty potatoes. There's nothing better! She used to say,

"How about if I just fry us some potatoes?"

If it was a cold day and we were feeling down—or even if we were in a good mood and felt like having something delicious and fun between the two of us. It was true comfort food, but it was also a moment of joyful camaraderie with my mom. To this day, if I feel like I need to cheer myself up, or if I want to show somebody I love them, I say,

"How about if I just fry us some potatoes?"

I'll slice some, heat up the skillet, and the day turns around no matter what. It's not so hard to make, but it's an unforgettable treat!

Crispy Hot Salty Potatoes

INGREDIENTS (FOR 2)

1 Tbsp extra-virgin olive oil

½ medium yellow onion, sliced into thin half moons

Salt

1 large Idaho potato, sliced into thin coins

1 Tbsp unsalted butter

METHOD OF PREPARATION

1. Place a large sauté pan on medium heat.

2. Add the oil. When shimmering, add the onions, and season with salt, tossing a couple of times to coat with oil. Cook for 2 minutes.

3. Place the potatoes in the pan, roughly in a single layer, and season liberally with salt. Cook for 3 to 4 minutes.

4. Add the butter to the pan, and let foam. Cook for another 5 minutes, tossing once or twice to keep things cooking evenly.

5. When the potatoes are well-browned and crispy, turn out onto a plate and devour.

For the Record by Meshell Ndegeocello

I had finished the release cycle of my second album, *Peace Beyond Passion*, and it didn't chart as well as "If That's Your Boyfriend," but there was a cover that did really well. There were some signs the label wasn't sure what to do with me. Madonna's brother, who I loved, had persuaded me he should direct my next video, and I thought I looked like a drag queen. I was pretty unapologetic about my Blackness, my queerness, and my androgyny, but they tried hard to make me more "marketable." Nevertheless, I was feeling really good. I was settling into LA life. The records were sounding good. I was feeling technically on top of my game. I was working on new music.

After my first two albums, David Gamson and I shared an amazing relationship as producer and artist. David taught me how to make music, how to eat well, how to make a good cup of coffee—he exposed me to so many different things. I was always excited to make music with him; it was just a good experience. We went into my next recording assuming that we would be the right combination for the new songs.

We started the record. I wrote "Loyalty," "Bitter," "Fool of Me," and he and I recorded those songs. We had a meeting with the head of the label and a couple other people. We go in, we play the record. That is one of the hardest things to do, and since then, when people ask me to check out something, I refuse to do it when they're in the room. Having been there, it's for the best not to do it with the artist.

I sat in the room, they listened to the music, no one had any sort of facial expression, and they just simply told me that this wasn't gonna work and to find a new producer. The head of the label went over to his stack of *Billboard* magazines and other industry periodicals and asked, "Who has the number one record? Let's call them." No relationship whatsoever. That didn't matter. That was just insulting. I think I got up and walked out of the meeting.

The label wanted a famous producer, and as this was happening, my friend Craig Street was getting kudos having just produced a number of successful albums. I trusted Craig already, so I brought him to LA, we do the whole dance with the

No one had ever said anything like that to me.

label, they're happy, I'm happy, we do the meeting, and we talk about what's left of the budget. After recording with David, and the time writing and just living in LA, there was a fraction of the budget left. That's a whole other story.

We had to make the album really quickly, but it was a great experience, with musicians who became my friends and family to this day. We were in a studio in the Valley that was very brown, like the brown crayon, I remember that. I cooked for the band and made coffee during breaks. It was a nourishing time, and I felt great about the music.

When I handed it in, the label listened and the marketing team told me they "couldn't sell it." The head of the label asked me why I didn't make Black music and told me that I should make a "Black record." No one had ever said anything like that to me. I'd gotten criticism before, feedback and suggestions, but to say that I did not make Black music was really hard to hear. I was crushed. It sent me into quite a spiral, a deeply difficult and depressing summer. The toxicity of that experience contaminated my days for a long time.

By the time it came out, I think the label and I were mutually disenchanted. The album was titled *Bitter*, and it was released with barely any promotion. The good news is that it clarified my own priorities: friendship, musical integrity, people and partners that made me better, clean food and decent coffee. Maybe I wasn't ever going to succeed at being the most marketable and maybe it would cost me fame and fortune, but I would make what I wanted to make.

A *Soft Spot* by Alex Wagner

JOURNALIST

I graduated from college in 1999 and all of my friends, en masse, decided to move to New York, a city that sounded hard as hell to live in. I'd visited Los Angeles one spring break, and here was a city that appeared to have miles of donut shops and innumerable vintage cars, as well as apartments that college graduates could actually afford. I moved there—and smugly noted to all of my New York friends that, though shitty, my apartment complex had a swimming pool. It was good for a while, but then I got another job—and then another, one that requested I relocate back to New York. Two years at that point seemed like a lifetime in Los Angeles, and so the move back east was welcome. There were still college friends available as roommates, and I found my favorite one of them and we moved in together—to what I now recognize as an unbearably shitty, roach-infested dungeon on the as-yet ungentrified Lower East Side. We loved it, I think.

My new job was conveniently located thirteen blocks from where I lived, and, inconveniently, paid me an incredibly low salary, so I was in the habit of packing my lunch for work each day. The Whole Foods Revolution had not yet begun, and so most of my food shopping was done at the bodega or—if I was feeling ambitious—at the "fancy" grocery store on Elizabeth Street, across the invisible poverty demarcation line of the Bowery. Here I could buy sliced whole-wheat bread, which I then used to make sandwiches. I had a soft spot for Italian-style tuna salad, and regularly made a lunch with canned tuna, olive oil, mustard, and black olives on the fancy whole-wheat bread from across the Bowery—which is what I had packed for myself on the morning of September 11, 2001.

That day was the Democratic mayoral primary in New York City, which I remember vividly because I left the dungeon and could not make any calls on my Motorola flip phone as I headed out to vote. I had no television, and there was no Twitter. The only thing I had was an unretrievable voice mail from my mother, who was living thousands of miles away from me, watching the horror unfold on her television at home. A homeless woman on my doorstep told me I'd need to get a refund from my phone carrier for today, "because of the planes." She pointed up to the sky, and I saw the black smoke of disaster curling in the blue—but because this was New York City, where chaos is commonplace,

I assumed it was just something awful but not cataclysmically so, and went on with my day.

I stopped at my polling place on my way to work, I voted in the primary, and I continued my walk to work, sandwich in hand. It was only when I arrived at the office that I realized we were under actual terrorist attack: We were close enough to Ground Zero to hear the screams of people when the towers fell. A few hours later, the street in front of our office was filled with dust-covered traders and secretaries and managing partners walking back uptown, like zombies. I remember the feeling of helplessness and vulnerability that day, but also how hard it was to grapple with the enormity of this hell, to process what was unfolding. Mostly, I remember because while I knew enough to go back to our apartment and pack some things (I knew I wouldn't be coming back for a while), I also couldn't figure out what to do with myself, how to recalibrate for the new reality we had all been thrust into. And so, that afternoon, around lunchtime, back in the dark of that terrible apartment, I opened my tinfoil-wrapped Italian tuna sandwich—a vestige of the old New York from just a few hours earlier—and ate it.

Tuna Salad Sandwich

INGREDIENTS (FOR 1)

5 oz [150 g] canned tuna, drained of oil or water

1 tsp mustard, preferably Dijon

1 Tbsp extra-virgin olive oil

2 tsp chopped black olives

Sliced whole-wheat bread

METHOD OF PREPARATION

1. In a mixing bowl, combine the tuna, mustard, oil and olives. Mix well.

2. Spread on bread and enjoy.

The only thing
I had was an
unretrievable
voice mail from
my mother.

Amidst a City Torn Apart by Ulla Johnson

FOUNDER AND FASHION DESIGNER

It was in the time of war, right before the bombing of Belgrade by NATO. My mom and entire maternal family were in Serbia as what I had always been taught was the miracle and magic of Yugoslavia crumbled around them. It had been several years since I had been back. I felt I had to go. Arrangements were made. I was to fly to Budapest and meet persons unspecified who would drive me and several others in a sprinter van through cover of darkness across the intervening miles and countless checkpoints into Belgrade.

In her typical fashion, my mother had not offered me much in the way of detail or encouragement. She had traveled this way herself, seemingly without a moment of fear or worry, and I was expected to do the same. It was a long journey. I cannot remember the number of hours we drove, or how many stops we made, but I do remember I was cold. My denim jacket wildly insufficient, I wrapped myself in whatever other bits and bobs a college girl embarks on such a trip with, which were few and certainly not the most appropriate.

I didn't chat with my fellow passengers much, and instead spent the time thinking of what awaited, how changed my city and family might be. In the end I arrived into my mother's eager arms and was rushed directly to my great-aunt's kitchen. She lived in an apartment that had once felt grand to me, with its proper dining room, fine crystal, and moldings. But the heart of the home had always been Lela's kitchen in the back with a small table featuring a shiny, patterned vinyl tablecloth where she would serve me and my mom and cousins the most delicious of meals—a combination of Austro-Hungarian haute cuisine and Bosnian comfort foods. I believe we ate burek that night—spiced ground meat wrapped in layers of phyllo dough and baked to perfection, and srpska salata consisting of finely chopped tomatoes and cucumbers and onions, and my very favorite dessert, šnenokle (also known as île flottante), a delicious concoction of meringue floating on crème anglaise. We were sad and scared and sorry for all that swirled about us, but this meal and this moment soothed us and, despite it all, laughter and comfort surrounded us in that cozy kitchen, twinkling amidst a city torn apart by conflict and terror.

Šnenokle

4 large eggs

Pinch of cream of tartar

4 ½ cups [1 L] whole milk

¼ cup [50 g] sugar

1 tsp vanilla extract

2 Tbsp all-purpose flour

METHOD OF PREPARATION

1. Separate the egg yolks from the whites. Reserve the yolks. In a mixing bowl of a stand up mixer, beat the egg whites until fluffy, then add the cream of tartar. Continue to mix on high speed until you achieve stiff peaks.

2. In a wide saucepan, heat the milk until it is just under a boil, approximately 200°F [95°C].

3. Using a large tablespoon, scoop egg-shaped dumplings from your egg white mixture and drop into your simmering milk. Cook for 30 seconds on the first side and flip. Cook for another 30 seconds, then transfer to a serving plate to cool. Repeat with the rest of the whipped whites, dipping the spoon into cold water between scoops.

4. Strain the milk to remove any egg white left over from cooking. Return the strained milk to the saucepan.

5. In a separate bowl, vigorously whip the egg yolks, sugar, and vanilla until pale and fluffy. Add the flour and mix well.

6. Add the egg yolk and flour mixture to the milk and cook over low heat, stirring constantly, until the mixture thickens enough to coat the back of a spoon, 5 to 7 minutes.

7. Pour the thickened milk into shallow bowls and float the meringue dumplings on top.

When the Rims Went Down
by Bobbito García aka Kool Bob Love

DJ/PRODUCER, FILMMAKER, AUTHOR, BALLPLAYER

Alison Riley: Do you cook?

Bobbito García: I do cook. I cook, but if you took all the cooking I have done in my life—my whole life—it would not equal the amount of cooking I did in 2020.

In my brain, the pandemic brought me to the "we are at war" place, and I had to survive. I am blessed that my immune system is strong, but I thought, "If I am going to survive this, I need to be as healthy as possible." I was eating 100 percent plant based, and I started jumping rope plus running stairs again as if I were back in college training for b-ball.

I had been toying with being a vegan for probably twenty years. I was introduced to it way back then, and probably in these last two years I had been 70 to 75 percent vegan. I was loving how the food treated my body, and what it meant for the environment, for independent farmers, for pushing forward positive change and anti-corporate, anti-capitalist ideals. Anyway, March 11, 2020, came along and the stay-at-home orders started and I didn't have to be outside or on the road or overseas, opting for something quick and unhealthy. I could control the food narrative on a daily basis, and it became much more plausible to reach that goal of being plant based.

There was a series of deaths in my family in March, April, and May. It was heavy. I couldn't go to funerals, or go hug my mother. And then my son's mother was affected by COVID, so I was cooking for her, bringing her dishes on a little green table, then leaving them outside her door. She wound up being in quarantine for thirty-seven days.

You could combine all the f*ckin' scrambled eggs I've made in my life, all the pancakes—they don't equal the cooking I did that month. I was making her three meals a day, healing foods and soups. Maybe not what my son and I were eating— and what my son eats I don't always want to eat, so, in the course of one day, I was

But the dishes, the dishes, the f*ckin dishes.

sometimes making seven to nine meals. The cooking wasn't so bad—it was kind of a joy. I felt like I was helping someone heal, taking care of my son, taking care of myself. But the dishes, the dishes, the f*ckin dishes. The cleaning up afterward, the salt on the counter, the floor has to be wiped up, the garbage has to be taken out more often 'cause there's more food. Endless.

But the event that really crushed me was the week the parks and recreation department took the rims down. In my whole life, basketball has been my source of joy, my safe space, and when the rims went down it felt like the most unthinkable horror film ever. Couldn't go to gyms, couldn't be indoors, only safe if we're outdoors, mask on, distance, but damn, I can't even shoot basketball now . . . F*ck me.

However tempting, I wasn't trying to go to a pizza shop during all this. The nearest shop was a mile and change walk, and I am vegan now, so I started making homemade vegan pizza with sweet potato wraps instead of dough, with the pizza sauce, and the shredded vegan mozzarella, and then I would throw spinach on top, or chop up squash or zucchini, or throw broccolini on top, put my little oregano, sprinkle olive oil, my garlic powder, and everything you'd see at the pizza shop. Well . . . not everything. I can't mess with the red pepper flakes, but everything else, touch of salt and pepper. It would not only feel good 'cause it was a healthy meal but it was that reminder of New York, pizza outside, bugging out, at the shop, walking with a slice with oil dripping out on your shoelaces, and you'd be like . . . "Dag!"

The Simplicity of Congee by LinYee Yuan

EDITOR, *MOLD MAGAZINE*

My cat was dying. For four days, my time was marked by hand feeding, constant fretting, and trips to the vet for bloodwork and a cocktail of pills. On the winter solstice, the longest night of the year, I woke up at 4 a.m. with the urge to make congee. The rice porridge is my ultimate comfort food, a humble bowl that sends warm waves of energy radiating out from my core. My favorite version, made with chicken stock or the leftover chicken bones from a roast, would be a fitting tribute to my poultry-loving cat.

Like its less brothy twin, steamed rice, congee is more a vehicle for other textures and flavors. My ideal bowl would start my day, a warming porridge topped with fluffy scrambled eggs, pillowy pork floss, the sweet and tart tang of soy cucumber pickles, funky chili bamboo, bright green onions, and a generous slick of crispy, garlicky, chili oil. A side of you tiao, a long length of fried dough meant to be torn in two and dipped into the congee or a warm bowl of soy milk, is a nice treat when having congee at a restaurant, but optional.

The warmth and versatility of porridge is a comforting hug that settles the stomach while filling it up. When the world around me seems tenuous at best, comfort can be found in the straightforward simplicity of congee.

When the world around me seems tenuous at best, comfort can be found.

Chicken Congee for Oski

1 cup [200 g] short-grain white rice

8 cups [2 L] chicken stock

Salt and white pepper

Aromatics like ginger, carrots, sweet potatoes, and other spices can be used but not necessary

1. Rinse and drain the rice once or twice with running water to remove any impurities.

2. Add the rice and chicken stock to a large pot. Bring to a boil over high heat, partially cover the pot, and turn down the heat to medium-low to maintain a simmer. Stir occasionally to make sure the rice isn't sticking together or to the bottom of the pot.

3. The congee is done when the rice has bloomed and incorporated the stock, about 1½ to 2 hours. It should have the consistency of oatmeal.

4. Season with salt and white pepper (if you have it!) to taste. Serve with a mix of savory, crispy, umami toppings of your choice.

Indestructible Pea Soup by Brian Lehrer

HOST, *THE BRIAN LEHRER SHOW*, WNYC RADIO

I tend to eat and cook very simply and am not the person to turn to for recipes, believe me. In fact, I recommend that you skip this page and go on to the next person.

For those of you who chose to read on anyway, here's another thing about me that's not worth knowing: In the early days of the pandemic, I was figuring out how to safely get food into my apartment, like everybody else, but then I had this dental problem—I'll spare you those details—that resulted in an extraction and the beginning of the process for an implant. (Take this as another opportunity to flee if you'd like.)

Dental work, of course, is not the most fun you'd ever have to begin with, but in the pandemic, I was less concerned about some dumb tooth that I could get replaced than I was petrified by sitting with my mouth unmasked and wide open for someone to mess around in for an hour or so who was not from my household, and had no vaccine passport for me to ask for yet. I wondered about that thing I had just learned about how N95s don't work all that well on health care workers if they're not individually fitted. Did this solo practitioner dental office know how to do that? At least I wasn't in Texas, I thought at the time, where dentists might have the right to exercise personal freedom and not wear a mask at all. They are very pro-choice about what to be pro-choice about down there, if you know what I mean.

It all turned out fine. But it put me on soft food for the transition, and gave me a craving for split-pea soup. News flash: The split-pea soup in a can you might have grown up with gives you a month's worth of sodium. So I consulted with a friend who knows how to turn on a stove better than I do, and got a recipe for a simple and smooth, deliciously thick split-pea soup. Best served really hot, and don't skimp on the pepper if pea soup is usually too bland for you.

A good thing for me about split peas is that they are virtually indestructible. They can't break, like those eggs I thought I was clever getting delivered rather

Dental work, of course, is not the most fun you'd ever have to begin with.

than going into a store. Also, like with many soup bases, you can add veggies or whatever you like to help make it a meal. Chopped carrots are one common choice. Also, you can make pea soup thicker or thinner—I go for about as thick as it can still be called soup—depending on how much water you add. First sauté some curry powder in olive oil over low heat. Then stir in some crushed garlic, add the water and peas, and liven it up with that sprinkle of fresh ground pepper to taste. Between the pea soup and the automatic permission to have a lot of ice cream that comes with a soft-food diet, you can still have fun eating during your next dental recovery. And if you need another recipe, just let me know and I'll ask another friend. Personally, I'm just about out.

A G&T for the Down & Out
by Gabrielle Hamilton

CHEF, OWNER OF PRUNE RESTAURANT

When I was sixteen, I moved to NYC with $230 in high school graduation gifts and a large jar of loose change, and I survived on this for months until I could find a job. I swiped handfuls of ketchup packets from McDonald's to make spaghetti sauce. I bought canned sardines at the bodega for 35 cents each. And wherever there was an advertised happy hour with free hot food, I laid my stacks of quarters onto the bar and ordered two bottles of the cheapest beer they had. I always left a separate stack of quarters to tip the unsmiling bartender, but even so, he seethed his disdain as he set the little paper plate in front of me that came with the qualifying two-drink minimum. Those complimentary Buffalo wings and that watery beer were sometimes my only meal in a span of days.

I still love a can of sardines—with Triscuit crackers and Dijon mustard—and am not above an occasional Buffalo wing when the craving strikes. But my down-and-outs now require a bracing and crisp gin and tonic. I just can't be consoled by piss-water beer anymore.

It's a 50/50 gin-tonic ratio. Keep the Tanqueray in the freezer so it pours like syrup. Use solid ice cubes that won't water down the "medicine." Keep the tonic refrigerated, too, and tally the giant squeeze of lime as part of the 50 percent mixer, not the 50 percent gin, obviously. Cold, crisp, effervescent, and pretty hefty, it's a real mood elevator. If you bring the drink to your lips for a first sip and notice that in your distracted despondency you forgot to peel off the little barcode sticker on the hunk of lime now floating in the ice, consider it extra good luck, as I do.

Gin and Tonic

INGREDIENTS (FOR 1)

3 oz [90 ml] Tanqueray gin, kept in the freezer

2½ oz [75 ml] Fever Tree Refreshingly Light tonic water, refrigerated

¼ juicy lime, fully squeezed into the drink

Solid cube ice

METHOD OF PREPARATION

1. Combine all ingredients and stir. Serve.

I just can't be consoled by piss-water beer anymore.

If Martha Stewart Only Knew!
by Richard Christiansen

FOUNDER OF CHANDELIER CREATIVE, FLAMINGO ESTATE, OWL BUREAU

I was fishing with friends on a commercial fishing trawler in the Long Island Sound, heading toward Block Island. The water was so choppy, and the cell service was, too. Suddenly, I got a message that Martha Stewart would be coming over for dinner.

We pulled the lines in and scrambled to get back to land. The house was a disaster after a string of parties, and Martha would be aghast at its condition. The trawler and its brooding, whiskey-smelling crew with their huge leathery hands dropped us off in the harbor near my place in Montauk, and we swam ashore. Makes me laugh now to think of it, these gruff Montauk fishermen watching this gaggle of gays scrambling ashore to clean the house for Martha Stewart—high alert on the high seas!

Back at home, we frantically cleaned from top to bottom, throwing anything and everything into the cupboards and closets with wild abandon, just beating the clock as Martha finally arrived. Always game for conversation and cocktails, we chatted up Martha late into the night. For dinner, we prepared the fresh sea bass we'd caught. Of course, Martha said that it needed some salt.

Exhausted from the day with the evening successfully behind us and Martha out the door, I was ready to relax. Looking for a T-shirt, I opened the bedroom armoire only to unleash an avalanche of dirty dishes, bread loaves, mail, casserole pans—you name it—from among the clothes. If Martha only knew!

Suddenly,
I got a message
that Martha
Stewart would
be coming
over for dinner.

Simple Roasted Striped Bass

INGREDIENTS (FOR 4)

Four 6 oz [170 g] striped bass fillets, skin on

Kosher salt

Extra-virgin olive oil

METHOD OF PREPARATION

1. Preheat the oven to 300°F [180°C].

2. With paper towels, pat the fillets dry. With a very sharp knife, score two small slits in the skin of each piece. Do not cut from edge to edge or cut too deep.

3. Preheat a large nonstick or well-seasoned cast-iron pan over medium-high heat. Generously season each fillet on both sides with salt.

4. When the pan is hot, add some olive oil. Place one fillet skin side down. Press lightly with a spatula to brown the skin. Repeat with the other fillets.

5. When the edges of the fish start to brown slightly, slide the entire pan into the oven. After 8 to 10 minutes, check your fish. The sides should be a nice white while the top is just slightly opaque. Remove the pan from the oven and, using a stiff spatula, slide under the skin and flip the fillets. Let them rest in the pan for 5 minutes to ensure cooking on the flesh side; when tested with a meat thermometer, the fish should reach 120°F [50°C].

6. Transfer to a paper towel–lined plate to absorb leftover cooking oil.

7. Serve with lemon wedges or a simple salad.

Scared & Horny Sandwich by Fran Tirado

WRITER, PRODUCER, COHOST OF *FOOD 4 THOT*

Coming from a Chicana-Boricua diaspora, you'd think my parents would've passed more of our Latinx culinary tradition down to me. Yet, all I really got was this sandwich "recipe." As the oral history goes, my parents (then twenty-two and twenty-three) were dirt broke and living together for the first time in a one-bedroom apartment. Fresh off their honeymoon, their lives were turned upside down with the news of their first child (moi), who they were neither emotionally nor financially prepared for. The first night they spent together as a newlywed couple in their apartment, they ate a cold rotisserie chicken sandwich with a baguette, avocado, and lime—a meal that cost less than $10 at most grocery stores.

This simple sandwich became my favorite growing up, so much so that I would request it on my birthday. Now, I return to it as a comfort food when I am scared, horny, or both, which is often. I ate this sandwich the day my first boyfriend in New York broke up with me. It was my first relationship in four years and I had uncharacteristically put myself out there only to be totally rejected (though he did later call to tell me to get tested because he might've given me gonorrhea). That day, I'd also managed to eat shit stepping off an MTA bus in front of a crowd of pedestrians, badly bloodying up my knees and palms. New to the city, without friends, bandaged up, and crying alone in my first dirt-broke apartment, I wondered if I could handle the pressure of making it on my own. Heartbroken, I made myself this sandwich to feel something familiar. It satiated all my needs and staved off my scaries/horniness 'til another day.

I return to it as a comfort food when I am scared, horny, or both, which is often.

Rotisserie Chicken Sandwich

This is my version, updated slightly to accommodate my fanciness.

1 fresh French baguette

2 Tbsp unsalted butter

Whole-grain mustard

2 oz [50 g] sharp Cheddar cheese, thinly sliced

½ ripe avocado, minced

Coarse salt and freshly ground black pepper

Red pepper flakes

2 oz [50 g] soft goat cheese

1 handful baby kale

¼ store-bought rotisserie chicken, shredded

½ lime

Do I really need to "follow instructions" for this recipe, you may be thinking? It's a sandwich, not rocket science. Where I am not a deli essentialist, I am a Virgo moon and do have a specific way of putting this together if you care to follow along.

Slice open the baguette lengthwise with a serrated knife and separate into two parts. Removing the butt of the baguette, cut the desired portion of bread (I personally go for a hand-sized sandwich). Spread half the butter onto both sides of the bread slices and set on either side of a cutting board. On one side, spread the desired amount of mustard, layering the Cheddar cheese on top. Also on that side, spread avocado and sprinkle with salt, pepper, and red pepper flakes. This specific layering prevents the bread from absorbing the moisture of the avocado and creates optimal flavor combinations with Cheddar-mustard and Cheddar-avo.

On the other side, spread the goat cheese and top with the baby kale. Pile as much rotisserie chicken as can fit onto the kale side, then squeeze the lime half (more or less) onto the shredded chicken until evenly moistened. Again, this creates optimal taste combos, and kale prevents the lime from absorbing into the bread. Using a spatula, flip the avocado side carefully onto the chicken side. Melt the remaining butter in a skillet over medium-low heat. Transfer the sandwich to the skillet and grill until golden brown, or a little more. Flip and grill until the Cheddar cheese has completely melted.

If exceedingly scared/horny, this sandwich is just as good skipping the grill and eaten cold.

Security Pizza by Becca Blackwell

PERFORMER, WRITER

When I was little, I thought that girls who were fat didn't get molested. I had a paper route, so I had cash and I figured out how to order pizza. I would keep pizzas under my bed so I could eat them, get fat, and be safe.

And since I was assigned a vagina at birth, I would spend the rest of my life thinking I was fat since so much of a woman's value is based on her body and her attractiveness to men. Add that to being a soft-looking butch, and I never could find any sense of power internally. I had conflicting systems running inside of me. I felt more masculine, but I never felt like a man. All of which is probably why I never felt like I fit in. But eventually queerness will expand, my place will appear, and we will all be LGBTQIABCDEFGHIJKLMNOPQRSTUVWXYZ.

Here's how I get pizza now:

Preheat the oven to 450°F [230°C]. Basic crust recipe: In a large bowl, mix one ¼ oz [7 g] package of yeast, 1 cup [240 ml] of warm water, and 1 tsp of sugar together. Let sit until creamy, 8 to 10 minutes. Then add 2½ cups [350 g] of flour, 2 Tbsp of olive oil, and 1 tsp of salt. Beat with a hand mixer or a wooden spoon until smooth. Let sit for at least 5 minutes. Roll out into rounds or whatever shape you like pizza in.

My personal favorite topping is a poor man's pesto, which is 1 bunch of parsley and 1 bunch of cilantro blended with garlic, salt, olive oil, and pepitas (or almonds or walnuts work if you're rich). If I have fresh Parm, I'll throw it in. I put a thick layer on the dough and then add sliced Brussels sprouts that I have precooked in olive oil and garlic. Put a little of that Parm on and shove it in the oven. If I've got dough left over or want another pizza, I use any leftover pesto and then I do a chorizo and broccoli rabe (I always add fresh garlic to the broccoli rabe when cooking). Put some of that fresh Parm on and goddamn. Each pizza needs about 12 to 15 minutes depending on how crispy you like it. Salt is your friend.

Eventually, queerness will expand and we will all be LGBTQIABC DEFGHIJKLM NOPQRSTUV WXYZ.

Staples by Rachel McKibbens

POET, WITCH, MAMA

Any time one of my uncles had a court appearance, my grandmother would listen to the guttural ballads of Chavela Vargas as she stirred a cauldron of pintos over the stove. Instead of singing along, she'd chase each lyric with "MY BOY! MY BOY! MY POOR BOY!" Melodrama, the first ingredient.

A staple for every Mexican family, beans are shamefully overlooked due to their simplicity, but it is in the careful ritual of their preparation that you notice the soft pings of love and grief ricocheting off the heart's interior. If you've grown up in a house of the habitually incarcerated, you know it has its own kind of weather: rising steam from the boiling water humidifies the kitchen, peeling the wallpaper eventually. It coats the kitchen windows where children, wallowing in their freedom, can draw primitive little :(with curious fingers—telegrams of grief for each passerby. Uncle Vinny's sentence for gun possession meant a plastic bag slit open, dried beans cackling onto the linoleum tabletop. The silence we held as we sifted out the misshapen rejects or small stones became the second ingredient.

Over the years, as each sentence elongated a son's absence, my grandmother taught me the hand is the best measuring cup, tears an adequate response to both cash bail and severed onions. When Uncle Phillip got clipped for his third strike, it was a slow pot of beans that soothed our family. Breakfast, lunch, and dinner. Tiny jalapeño bits and garlic were added once Gilbert's parole officer found out he OD'd. Locked up again for addiction. More salt, 'til the water becomes gray. Cayenne for the daughter he never met.

I now own a restaurant in Upstate New York, far from the streets of Southern California where I grew up. My grandmother's beans are on the menu, an automatic side dish to our tacos. Often, they come back to the kitchen, untouched, and I scrape them into the trash, wash the dish, and keep it moving. But every once in a while, someone will ask, "Who made the beans?" and I come out to greet them, because it's always someone who gets it. "They taste like my grandmama's beans!" or "These remind me of my favorite beans from El Pollo Loco! I had to meet the person who made these. You from Cali?" And always, always, I say, yes,

I'm from Santa Ana. Mi barrio. My grandmother taught me how to make them. But she died with the tamale recipe. Never shared it. She needed something to stay hers.

Spicy Pinto Beans

INGREDIENTS (FOR 4)

½ cup [70 g] diced onion

½ cup [60 g] seeded and diced jalapeño

2 Tbsp minced garlic

2 Tbsp garlic powder

1 Tbsp cayenne pepper

One 1 lb [455 g] bag dried pinto beans

Salt

METHOD OF PREPARATION

1. Fill a large pot with water to about 2 in [5 cm] below the rim. Add the onion, jalapeño, minced garlic, garlic powder, and cayenne to the water, but do not add the salt. I mean it, do NOT add the salt! Bring to a boil over high heat.

2. While waiting for the water to boil, empty the beans into a bowl and sort out any stones or oddities. Add the sorted beans to the boiling water, lower the heat, and allow to simmer until the water darkens and becomes broth-like. Stir occasionally.

3. The beans will take a couple of hours to become tender. Optionally, add salt to the water once they are soft. If added earlier in the cooking process, the beans will become tough. I am a salty bitch and salt the hell out of them. Your call!

4. DO NOT DRAIN THE WATER.

5. Serve in a bowl with a large flour tortilla, folded into a quarter.

Melodrama, the first ingredient.

Mother of Invention by Jacqueline Woodson

AUTHOR

Chicken . . . again.

My mom couldn't cook. She tried. We didn't starve. We circled the table every evening not so much dreading what was put down in front of us, but with an ennui four kids in Brooklyn by way of the South should never have to bring to the dinner table. I always chose the window seat. There was a gutter drain just outside of it, and this is where so much of my dinner ended up. Once, as a child, I put liver and onions in my pocket and later had to lie away the cause of the grease stains. Lumpy grits. Thick, undercooked Aunt Jemima pancakes, pink-boned chicken, cube steaks like chewing gum, dry and blistered porgies—the list went on and on. My sister, younger brother, and I were underweight. My older brother, existing on a diet of mayonnaise sandwiches, junk food, and bodega heroes, was not. Still, we survived. I credit a lot of that survival to my best friend Maria's mother. Maria lived three doors away and her mother pulled magic out of her refrigerator and kitchen cabinets—rice and chicken stews (arroz con pollo), pigeon peas with bits of beef, deep-fried pastalitos, chicken soups—yes, it was still chicken—but it . . . *wasn't.*

And we survived too because my grandmother joined us in Brooklyn when we were still young and took over the cooking. A Southern woman to the core, my grandmother was both a gardener and a chef. She and my mother turned our backyard into a world of milk crates sprouting collards, lettuces, tomatoes, cucumbers, and herbs. My mother planted an apple and a pear tree that, all these years later, still bear fruit. Our world became Southern fried chicken and fried sweet potato pies. It became collards cooked with smoked turkey wings and macaroni and cheese casseroles. It became homemade ice cream and ambrosia, pancakes from scratch with caramelized bananas. It became a world I walked into and discovered my own love of silent time in the kitchen, figuring out how to turn the old into new (chicken seemed to always be on sale somewhere in the Bushwick of my childhood and because of that, we ate it—a LOT!).

Now when I want to revisit that childhood—from my grandmother's kitchen to Maria's mother's—this is the dish I find myself making.

A Black Girl's Puerto Rican Chicken Stew

Here's the thing about sofrito—make a whole bunch, freeze it in ice cube trays, and pop a few cubes out to season just about anything you're cooking—from beans to greens to meats.

Sofrito

INGREDIENTS (1 CUP)

8 garlic cloves, roughly chopped

1 large yellow onion, cut into eighths

1 red bell pepper, seeded and cut into quarters or eighths

1 green bell pepper, seeded and cut into quarters or eighths

1 bunch cilantro, rinsed and roughly chopped

½ cup [120 ml] olive oil

2 Tbsp salt

METHOD OF PREPARATION

1. Put the garlic in a food processor and pulse until finely chopped.

2. Add the onion, bell peppers, and cilantro and pulse until finely chopped, almost like salsa. Add the oil and salt and process briefly until incorporated.

3. Reserve or freeze.

Chicken Stew

2 Tbsp olive oil

6 to 8 bone-in chicken thighs

Salt and freshly ground black pepper

1 yellow onion, roughly chopped

2 garlic cloves, chopped

3 to 4 Tbsp sofrito (recipe precedes)

1 bay leaf

2 Tbsp cumin

1 Tbsp onion powder

1 Tbsp garlic powder

1 Tbsp dried oregano

1 tsp paprika

1 tsp turmeric

1½ cups [360 ml] chicken broth

One 6 oz [170 g] can crushed tomatoes (NOT with basil— I sometimes make that mistake!)

1 Tbsp tomato paste

½ cup [120 ml] water

1. In a Dutch oven over medium, heat the olive oil. Season the chicken with salt and pepper, add to the pot, and brown on both sides, then set aside on a plate (if it seems like a lot of oil left in the pan, drain a little off).

2. In the same pan, sauté the onion and garlic for about 2 minutes.

3. Add the sofrito. Cook—if frozen—until melted. If fresh, cook for about 3 minutes. Add the bay leaf, cumin, onion powder, garlic powder, oregano, paprika, and turmeric. Sauté for a minute but don't let the spices burn.

4. Add the chicken and its juices.

5. Add the chicken broth, crushed tomatoes, and tomato paste. Bring to a boil.

6. Lower the heat, sample and adjust to taste, and cook for 40 to 50 minutes, partially covered. If the liquid looks low, add the water.

7. For the last 15 minutes or so, cook uncovered over low heat. You want the chicken falling off the bone.

Zigni to Warm My Heart by Raul Lopez

CREATIVE DIRECTOR OF LUAR

My friend's mom, Florina, invited me to Easter brunch at her home during a very difficult moment. Two days before, I lost my cousin to a sudden illness. Florina told me I had to come, and promised she would make something that would warm my heart after all the pain.

Around her table, Florina explained that, as a child in Sudan, her mom would make zigni, an Eritrean dish, for Easter day. Florina is Egyptian and Sudanese. She said she recreates the foods from Africa and her childhood because they are rich in flavor, spices, memories, and love. Zigni was all of those things; it was iconic in flavor and unforgettable in my heart.

Zigni

INGREDIENTS (FOR 4)

2 Tbsp [30 ml] canola oil

1 lb [455 g] onions, chopped

1½ Tbsp berbere spice

1 lb [455 g] stew meat (beef is traditional but chicken thighs or lamb shoulder works), cubed

⅓ cup [80 g] tomato paste

1 cup [240 ml] water

One 16 oz [455 g] can crushed tomatoes

2 hard-boiled eggs, peeled and quartered

METHOD OF PREPARATION

1. Place a pan large enough to hold the meat over medium-high heat. Add the oil and onion and cook until lightly browned.

2. Add the berbere and cook for 2 minutes.

3. Turn the heat up slightly and add the cubed meat. Stir well and cook for 5 minutes.

4. Add the tomato paste and cook for 1 minute. Add the water, then add the tomatoes.

5. Turn the heat down to low and cover. Simmer for approximately 2 hours or until the meat is tender, stirring occasionally.

6. Serve, garnished with the hard-boiled egg.

Joy and Relief by Alba Clemente
THEATRICAL DESIGNER

As a Southern Italian, I know that food is the cure for everything. Food cures the body and the soul. Food is called for in happy celebrations and sad occasions. Sitting at a nicely set table in front of a good meal—preferably with family members or friends—is always a joy and a relief.

As a mother, I also know that once your children are fed, most of the work is done—for that day. But another one starts soon after. And another. But there was not an evening, raising our four children in New York City and having a pretty busy life, that we didn't have dinner all together. I loved them, but I have to say, it was a relief when they all went to college and I didn't have to cook seven days a week.

Pasta alla Puttanesca

INGREDIENTS (FOR 2)

Salt

¼ cup [60 ml] extra-virgin olive oil

2 garlic cloves

1 Controne, Calabrian, or cayenne chile pepper

10 kalamata olives, pitted

2 Tbsp capers, rinsed if salted

15 cherry tomatoes, or one small can whole peeled plum tomatoes, drained

4 oz [115 g] dried spaghetti

METHOD OF PREPARATION

1. Place a large pot of water on the stove. Salt generously and turn to high heat.

2. Place a sauté pan over medium heat, add the olive oil, and warm. Lightly crush the garlic and mince. Add the garlic, chile pepper, olives, and capers to the pan. Cook for 5 minutes.

3. Add the tomatoes and cook for an additional 15 minutes.

4. While the sauce simmers, cook the pasta. When the water comes to a rolling boil, add the pasta and lightly stir to separate the noodles. Cook according to the package instructions. Dried spaghetti usually takes 10 to 12 minutes.

5. When the pasta is cooked, strain. Don't rinse the noodles! Add the noodles to the sauce and toss for a few minutes.

6. Serve immediately.

A Dish to Hold the Love by Damani Baker

FILMMAKER

I come from a family of chefs. Louisiana is in my blood, food, and heart, but I learned to cook from my father, Prestin, who was from Denver, Colorado, and knew food was care. The type of care that meant sitting still, trout fishing at San Pablo Dam with packed lunches of fried bologna sandwiches, generic store-brand soda, and Fritos. After church, roasted chicken with canned beans and skillet cornbread.

On December 7, 2005, Prestin Levi Baker, my father, transitioned as lung cancer took over his body. December 7 is also my birthday. After his funeral, where the piano player played a few bars of Earth, Wind & Fire's "Fantasy" per my request, while sitting in his home, food began to arrive. The faces of every elder and ancestor whom I could remember rang the doorbell not to stay, not to speak too much, but to leave a dish knowing it would hold the love they felt for us in every bite. Their faces looked like the ones I remember in Geismar and Denver; they looked like the faces of both of my grandparents. They were faces of my mourning family, smiling at me like my father sitting on the shore, smiling at me without speaking, letting the sunflower seeds fall beneath us.

Aunt Shirley's Red Velvet Cake

INGREDIENTS
(FOR ONE TWO-TIERED
9 IN [23 CM] CAKE)

Nonstick cooking spray

2 large eggs

2 cups [480 ml] vegetable oil

1 cup [240 ml] buttermilk

3½ tsp vanilla extract

*2 cups [400 g] granulated
sugar*

*2 tsp Hershey's unsweetened
cocoa powder*

1 tsp baking soda

Pinch of salt

*2½ cups [350 g] all-purpose
flour*

*¼ cup [60 ml] red food
coloring*

*8 oz [230 g] Philadelphia
cream cheese, at room
temperature*

*½ cup [115 g] butter, at room
temperature*

*One 1 lb [455 g] box
confectioners' sugar*

Splash of milk

*½ cup [60 g] chopped pecans
[optional]*

METHOD OF PREPARATION

1. Preheat the oven to 350°F [180°C]. Spray two 9 in [23 cm] cake pans with nonstick cooking spray.

2. In a large bowl using a hand mixer, or in a stand mixer, beat the eggs, oil, buttermilk, and vanilla on medium speed until combined. Add the granulated sugar, cocoa powder, baking soda, and salt and beat until fully incorporated.

3. Add the flour, little by little, followed by the red food coloring. Mix until completely smooth.

4. Transfer the batter to the prepared pans, splitting evenly between the two.

5. Bake for 20 to 25 minutes, until a toothpick inserted in the center comes out clean. Let cool in the pans, then remove from the pans and transfer to a cooling rack.

6. In a large bowl with a hand mixer, or in a stand mixer, whip the cream cheese and butter together until smooth. Slowly add the confectioners' sugar and milk. Finish with three-fourths of the pecans, reserving the rest for decoration.

7. Frost the cooled cake, then sprinkle with the reserved pecans.

Spread Peanut Butter, Not Pain by Ron Finley

Alison Riley: So the reason you don't have any one story about a low point is because these aren't the memories you're trying to carry forward.

Ron Finley: I mean, I thought and thought and thought . . .

AR: No! Good for you if you're not carrying it forward.

RF: I'll tell you, though, I went to a Tony Robbins event and, you know, they have you walk on the coals, and people are crying. In one exercise, they want you to feel the pain, to get into the pain that you have. And I was trying—trying to feel the pain. I called over one of the event people and said I didn't think I was doing it right. She said just to be calm and feel whatever came. And I was trying to get into it, to find some pain. I mean, I am Black and I grew up in America; I got to have some pain. When it was over, and people shared all these horrible stories, I realized I am not holding on to any of that, I don't have that kind of pain. Seeing that, hearing that, it just let me know: I am not feeling it because I do not have it. I don't take that pain with me.

AR: I aspire to that.

RF: But what really came to mind is peanut butter. Peanut butter has always been my go-to when times were lean.

AR: Do you prefer it any way in particular?

RF: I make a hell of a peanut butter sandwich. Get some grilled challah with sautéed bananas, sautéed strawberries, PB, and then some strawberry jam. So you got this hot fruit with this hot, grilled soft bread.

AR: Ooh, grilled bread.

RF: You know, you go to places and you say I want the bread *grilled* and they give you *toasted*. People don't know the difference between grilled and

I am not holding on to any of that, I don't have that kind of pain.

toasted. I don't want it toasted. Toasted gets hard. Grilled still keeps some of the soft.

AR: Are you a chunky peanut butter person or do you like it smooth?

RF: I like mine smooth. It just spreads better. The peanuts, you know, they wind up . . .

AR: Ripping the bread!

Grilled Peanut Butter and Strawberry Jam Sandwich

INGREDIENTS (FOR 2)

1 pt [300 g] strawberries, sliced

2 ripe bananas, peeled and cut into coins

1 tsp sugar

Pinch of salt

1½ Tbsp butter

4 slices challah bread

Peanut butter

Strawberry jam

Note: you'll need to have a hot grill fired up or a cast-iron stove-top grill pan ready to go.

METHOD OF PREPARATION

1. In a bowl, gently mix the sliced strawberries and bananas with the sugar and salt.

2. Place a sauté pan that will comfortably fit all the fruit over medium-high heat. Add the butter. When it starts to bubble and foam, add the strawberries and bananas. Toss a couple of times to coat the fruit with the butter. Turn up the heat to high and cook the fruit until just tender, tossing or stirring frequently. Turn out the cooked fruit onto a plate and keep warm.

3. Place the challah slices on a hot grill or grill pan; you should hear an audible "hiss" when it hits. Let it cook on one side for 4 to 5 minutes, until you start to see browning on the edges. Using a spatula or tongs, take a peek and if you have solid grill marks, flip to the other side. Let cook for just 1 to 2 minutes. The goal here is to have a nice char on each face but steamed and soft throughout the interior.

4. To assemble, spread a layer of peanut butter on one half of your sandwich. Add a healthy dose of strawberry jam on the other half followed by a layer of the fruit. Top with the peanut butter slice of bread. Cut in half and serve warm.

My Favorite, Then and Now by Thundercat

BLACK MICHAEL MCDONALD IMPERSONATOR

I guess this would all go back to the days when my friend Austin Peralta was still alive. Right before he passed, I got a chance to take him to my favorite restaurant, Yoshinoya. It was somewhere my dad used to take me when I was a kid and it just kinda stuck with me throughout my whole life (it's still my favorite restaurant). Austin and I spent a whole lot of time together and were always picking at each other over things, be it big or small. He would challenge my reasoning on things all the time and made things interesting and fun. One drunken night, after a show somewhere in Hollywood around 3 or 4 a.m., we tried to find some food. He suggested tacos, and I got a bit excited about that, but then I was like, "Naw, let's go to Yoshinoya," and he was like, "What the hell is that?" I proceeded to tell him how important this restaurant was to me and we made the decision to go there.

My dad would get me the chicken bowl when I was a kid, but I would always get the beef bowl and the chicken bowl mixed up because I thought that the name of the bowl I was always eating was a beef bowl, as that was the name of the franchise. Austin wanted to see what all the fuss was about, so he insisted that he get the same thing I was getting. This was the order:

Extra-large chicken bowl
– extra chicken
– no veggies
– extra sauce

We took it back to my apartment but didn't wait to get in the house to eat. I didn't like the idea of eating outside on Crenshaw Boulevard at 4 a.m. with this crazy-ass piano player on a damn skateboard, drunk as hell, in front of my apartment complex, talking loud like we were still at a concert, waking up all the neighbors while we argue about Ron Carter. But this is one of my fondest memories of Austin. He died shortly after that at his young age. So all I can do now is remember the crazy skateboarding post-gig 4 a.m. dinner with one of my best friends ever to live and die, the great Austin Peralta.

Ceviche on the Stoop by Angelo Baque

CREATIVE DIRECTOR AND FOUNDER OF AWAKE NY

Angelo Baque: So, COVID. May. I felt like I hit a low point. I had been home alone, I don't think I had seen anybody, and I got really sick and tired of pasta and tacos. That was all I made for the first two months. Both of my parents are from Ecuador and the national dish is ceviche. Specifically, we're from the coast, from a city called Manta, and it's a huge port town, so if you're there you go to the malecón, the oceanfront, and you see big tuna being unloaded at like five in the morning. Culturally, how I grew up was: a lot of fish, a lot of seafood. If it swims, we ate it—that was the rule of thumb in our household.

My mother is the matriarch of the family, and her ceviche, her fish and shrimp ceviche, is incomparable. I have yet to taste anyone's, from restaurants to home cooking, five-star meals, whatever, of all the places I have been to, that compare to my mother's ceviche. I guess I was always afraid to even ask her to teach me, or to attempt, cause I thought she'd shut it down and kick me out of the kitchen.

I was missing my mom, I was alone, I was single at the time, and in all my feelings of deep patheticness and loneliness. It just dawned on me that I think I could do this, and I decided I was going to teach myself how to make this ceviche.

I was thinking, how's this any different from making salsa? I've seen my mother cut the limes, the onions, the cilantro. Some of her secrets are using adobo and salt and pepper, but there are no measurements, all this is just like making a potion. It's instinct and knowing how long to leave the shrimp in the lime and, of course, what's key is that you have to squeeze the limes, everything has to be from scratch, you can't use bottled lime juice.

There's a form of ceviche where you lightly boil the shrimp—less than like two to three minutes—and there are some dishes where the fish or the shrimp is cooked just by the lime, by the citrus. I prefer that—I don't like the flash boil because I feel like it overcooks the shrimp. That's me. It's the texture.

I worked myself up for it. I cut twenty-four limes. My mother put me to work as a kid, showing me this is how you squeeze limes, this is how to clean a shrimp.

It was like a form of meditation and therapy. Squeezing the limes and cleaning the shrimp—that is the memory of food. Not even the dish itself. It's all in the labor. Everything else is really easy.

Alison Riley: Do you have a recipe or do you just work off memory?

AB: Honestly, it's so simple and it is really about one's own personal taste. The key is getting that base right and letting it sit in that base. You gotta add a little filtered water to break down some of the acid 'cause sometimes straight lime juice is a little too acidic. But it's just salt, pepper, garlic, if you're feeling a little spicy throw in some jalapeños. What's key is the red onions, tomatoes, and the cilantro, which you add at the very end when you're ready to serve. You don't want that sitting in there.

AR: How was it?

AB: The first time, it was decent. And then over the summer, when people started to get more comfortable with seeing each other outside, I brought a bowl of ceviche to a friend's stoop in Bed Stuy to share. Everyone kept teasing me that I had a secret girlfriend who was cooking my shrimp ceviche for me. I ended up taking four or five batches to the stoop over the summer for special occasions.

This dish will always be connected to my family. When we got to eat ceviche, it was a treat, like a reward, because it is so labor intensive. To do it right, it is about a forty-eight-hour process. When I was in the second grade, I brought ceviche to elementary school for lunch, and I was so proud. This little white girl looked at me and said, "Your food stinks," and I was so embarrassed. I was embarrassed of the food, and though at the time I didn't realize it, I was feeling embarrassed of my culture—of being Ecuadorian. I thought, "You know, she's right. She's eating a fucking peanut butter and jelly sandwich, and that's what I should be eating." And I didn't really understand the layers of that trauma until I got older.

Now, being an adult and making the ceviche myself, and sharing that with all types of people—my friends, white, Black, brown, Latino—on my friend's stoop in Bed Stuy and everyone really enjoying it and appreciating it, I was like having this second life with this dish.

The real reward was making it for my aunt and my uncle and my mother, and they approved of it. They loved it. You know, if someone really loves you, they'll make you chifles, the plantain chips, which again, is not rocket science, it's just a pain in the ass 'cause you gotta thinly slice the platano. I made them chifles.

AR: Damn.

AB: Yeah! When I went to LA, I made chifles and ceviche for my friends and they were blown away 'cause they'd never had it like that. You know, in LA the culture is people eat ceviche on top of a tostada, but I cook white rice and the chifles and serve it on a bed of lettuce, in a little bowl. You scoop whatever's on the bottom with the lettuce. That's how I was taught. I got to pass on that ritual to my friends and share that with them. That's it.

An Overflow of Love and Plumbing
by Andrew Tarlow

RESTAURANT OWNER

The thing about always being busy is that it can often keep you from noticing the things that actually matter, and, in my case, it took a really disgusting situation to wake me up to what I couldn't see all along.

I met my wife, Kate, in June of 1998, the same month that my partner, Mark Firth, and I signed the lease on a then seventy-year-old dining car that was one block away from our loft on the South Side of Williamsburg. Kate was a new server at the Odeon, where I was bartending at the time, and, between working nights at the Odeon and the demo and construction at the diner every day, there would have been no chance for our new romance if she hadn't been more than willing to move in with us and join the rhythm of our days. She was an enthusiastic member of our team, if not very skilled in construction, and she made herself valuable by cooking us lunch down the street every day.

Days became weeks, weeks became months, and finally the big day had come and it was time to open the diner on New Year's Eve 1998/1999. That time is such a blur to me, waking up early for garbage pickup, prepping food all day for dinner service, working long services, and then closing the restaurant at 3 a.m. every night. Kate, Mark, our chef Caroline Fidanza, and I were there for it without a day off for many weeks, and those days were full of fun and joy, but no time for reflection.

One night, a couple of months into the winter of 1999, Kate, Mark, and I are in the full swing of another crazy service on a Saturday night when we get a shout from the kitchen that the plumbing is overflowing in the basement. I remember Kate was wearing a long gray skirt and these crimson velvet sandals that she had bought for herself in the South of France the year prior. She came barreling down the stairs to help with the septic mess and when she got to the bottom, her feet came out from under her and she landed fully in the mess, sandals fully trashed, but with a huge smile on her face, laughing as she looked up at me.

It was in that moment of filth and chaos, and maybe failure, that I fully felt the depth and breadth of her devotion to me. It hit me like a punch to the gut and tears came to my eyes. The weight of her young love knocked me out, and if not for a couple inches of sewage on the floor of the basement, I don't know how long it would have taken me to wake up to what was right in front of me for so many months. Twenty-three years have passed since that night and we have many more businesses and four children, and a very full life—good thing that running restaurants is ripe with daily mini-disasters so that too much time can never pass without getting that punch to the stomach to remind me of the love that is all around me.

Coq au Vin

INGREDIENTS (FOR 4)

Red table wine, enough to cover the chicken

6 bone-in, skin-on chicken legs and thighs

1 bunch of thyme

6 bay leaves

¼ cup [60 ml] extra-virgin olive oil

1 large onion, chopped

2 tsp garlic, minced

2 medium carrots, peeled and chopped

4 stalks celery, chopped

Salt and freshly ground black pepper

4 oz [115 g] bacon or salt pork, diced

2 Tbsp unsalted butter

2 large leeks, halved, cleaned, and cut into ½ in [12 mm] half-moons

12 oz [340 g] cremini mushrooms, thickly sliced

METHOD OF PREPARATION

1. Pour the red wine into a baking dish, add the chicken, and let soak. Make a bundle of herbs with the thyme and bay leaves and add to the wine. Marinate for at least an hour, up to 24 hours. Remove the chicken from the marinade and pat dry. Strain and reserve the marinade and herb sachet.

2. Preheat the oven to 250°F [120°C].

3. In a large pan, heat 2 Tbsp of the olive oil and cook the onion, garlic, carrots, and celery with pinches of salt until soft and translucent. Remove from the pan and reserve.

4. Season the chicken liberally with salt and black pepper. Add the chicken and bacon to the same pan, and brown on both sides. Reserve the crisped bacon on a warm plate.

5. Remove the chicken from the pan and wipe out the pan. Return the chicken and its juices to the pan and add the wine, herb sachet, and onion, carrot, and celery mixture. Cover the pan, transfer to the oven, and cook for 30 to 45 minutes, until cooked through. Reserve the chicken and strain the cooking liquid, discarding all the solids.

6. For the sauce, return the cooking liquid to the pan and cook down further, until slightly thickened. Remove from the heat and add 1 Tbsp of the butter to make the sauce glossy and creamy. Add the chicken to the sauce and keep in a warm place.

7. In a separate pan, warm the remaining 2 Tbsp olive oil and remaining 1 Tbsp butter and sauté the leeks and mushrooms until soft. Season while cooking with salt and pepper.

8. Combine the sauce, chicken, leeks, and mushrooms on a serving platter and garnish with the reserved bacon.

9. Serve with warm rice or buttered noodles.

How do you hold your weight?

Eighth Grade Memory Dance by Kyle Abraham

DANCER, CHOREOGRAPHER, ARTISTIC DIRECTOR

Close your eyes and envision a memory of your thirteen-year-old self.
How do you hold your weight?
Is your spine upright or hunched?
Remember the smell of the lunch room?

From those memories, soften both knees, and rotate your left hand and left foot.
Raise both shoulders and allow your right forearm to rise slightly;
leading from the back-hand side of your right wrist, open your right forearm
and step back on your right leg while curving/hollowing out your torso.
Send your left ring finger to the vulnerable space where your clavicle meets
your throat.
Your head shifts back to the left, diagonally.
Both knees turn inward, parallel.

Right knee and foot rotate onto the ball of the right foot.
Left fingers leave the throat and present a "stop" gesture to the back, diagonal
of your body.
Right knee turns in, while staying on the ball of the right foot. At the same time,
your right forearm inverts to have your fingertips pointing toward the floor.
Shift your left scapula toward your right and let that ripple through the right arm.
Right arm continues until your right fingertips are closer to your right eye and
your left ring finger touches your bottom lip.
From there, drop your head, and let your full body react (like a wave or ripple
through your spine).
Step forward on your left foot (in parallel).

With tension in both hands, push both hands past your waist.
Keeping the left hand where it is, allow your right shoulder blade to send your
right forearm to a 90-degree angle.
Leading with the right fingertips, sink in your head and chest, have your
left fingers meet your right in the center of your sternum, and close your eyes
(if you've opened them).

Keeping your eyes closed, continue to soften your sternum—hollowing out as much as you'd like . . . softening the knees in support (and to create more space for the back to settle).

Come back to your eighth grade memory.
How did you hold yourself?
How did a loved one hold you?
What did they smell like? What did their room smell like?
Keeping that memory present, and keeping your eyes closed, straighten both legs.
Keep your left hand connected to your sternum (allowing the fingers to spread more and the weight of your palm to lend heat and support to your heart and chest).
Slowly straighten your right arm.
Open your eyes . . . and feel present.

You show up at your concert with no pants on. How could you forget your pants?

De-Humiliating Muffins by Emily King

SINGER, COMPOSER

The invitation came.

"Come to the show tonight!"

Anita Baker sold out at Radio City Music Hall.

Of course I would go. I grew up listening to Ms. Baker on WBLS, the Quiet Storm. There was no voice like hers. So very identifiable.

My managers let us in the back way. We had VIP passes. "This is cool," I thought. A legend. Something I can talk about. Something I can remember. Great seats too. What are the chances?

Alicia Keys sat near us. Yeah, this IS cool. Anita sang and swayed through the night, sounding like a master of her voice. Soaring. Highs, lows. Restraint. My best friend Tierra was with me. Two-thirds into the concert, my manager shows up in the aisle shouting something. He seemed excited and nervous. From the look of his lips he was saying, "She wants you, come with me now!"

Just like that I'm eight years old at the talent show with adrenaline racing through my entire body. "Please, no." I thought.

"Nooooooo . . . no no no." I shook my head frantically. "I don't know her music. I don't know the songs!" I shouted.

"It's okay!" he replied. "Just sing the blues."

"What?" I winced. I didn't even know what that meant, but it somehow was enough to convince me.

I am not accustomed to improvising at other people's shows. I never do it. Even my own show is mapped out to the minute.

"Come now, she asked for you!" he said again. I looked at Tierra. She looked at me. Next thing I knew, we were both backstage.

"She's going to call you on after this song," the sound man said loudly and handed me a pair of in-ear monitors so I could hear the band.

"No monitors on stage," he said.

"Great," I thought. I pushed them into my ears and prayed that the music gods would feed me the right sounds.

There is a dream, a reccurring dream that performers have. You get called for a gig. You have to sing an Italian aria. You don't speak Italian and you've never sung opera before. The curtains rise, go! You show up at your concert with no pants on. How could you forget your pants? Boom, spotlight . . . you're up, kid, hit it! You slept in and missed the first half of the biggest show of your life and make it just before the ending; the audience hates you for being late. You open your mouth and nothing comes out . . . showtime, go!

The beauty of this dream is the waking up part. You sigh with relief and shake it off as you get up and make your morning coffee. "Ooof, thank heavens, it wasn't real." *sip*

This, however, was not that. Unfortunately. Radio City Music freaking Hall, sold-out show. My hometown. People I know and might recognize. Anita Baker, the legend. She calls me on stage to sing a verse of her song that I had never heard before. I repeat, NEVER HEARD BEFORE. Yes, I listened to WBLS but always casually and never with the intention of learning the words.

I looked down. Still wearing pants. "OK, you can do this, Em."

I'm on stage. I look at her, she points at me. "You take the verse!" she says and walks off the stage. I repeat, WALKS OFF THE STAGE. Holy shit, that is cool but please come back, Ms. Anita Baker. Come back please. It's me now and the band and a song I do not know and I can't hear the music because there is no sound in my in-ear monitors. No sound. A quiet stage. A full house. Trust me, I tried shaking myself awake several times.

"What now, Em?" I looked out at a confused and nervous audience. I called upon my show biz angels for help. "Are there chords playing?" "Try to hear them." "Talk to the audience. Say something!" I looked out into the crowd and shouted, "Give it up for Anita Baker!"

Crickets.

They'd been giving it up all night and now I was taking it all the way down. And I had no more planned material. I can remember trying to sing "ooohs" and "ahhhs" and two-stepping a lot. Clapping, trying to get the audience to clap. I was literally one step away from juggling. Juggling would have been better. This is bad, I thought. Really bad.

Is she coming back? I looked around. Am I left to finish out the show? What was I thinking? What was my manager thinking? You don't say no to Anita Baker is what we were both thinking. Why didn't I say no? I longed for that "no" now. I looked at the band. "Can we turn back time on this one please guys? To like three minutes ago so I can run out the back door? Thanks!" Then suddenly, in my peripheral vision, an angel appeared to rescue me from this very real nightmare. Ladies and gentlemen, Ms. Alicia Keys!

I applauded loudly and so did the audience. My heart exhaled in relief! A nervous, panicked gratitude. The crowd goes wild. A professional has arrived to save us both from entertainment hell! Thank the gods. The band was still playing the song I had been expected to sing. I looked over at Alicia. Did she know the words? Maybe not. But you'd never know it. "That's how you do it," I thought. "A fucking pro."

When the night was over, so was I. I was DONE. "This will never go away, Em. This is going to last forever on the internet," I told myself. Shame and humiliation just a click away for all of eternity, enjoy! A reminder of the night I let down R&B and Anita Baker and myself. Upset with my inability to say "No." Upset that this recurring dream had made its way into my dimension. Some glitch in the system, I suppose.

We stuck around after the show. I desperately looked for redeeming qualities in the night, knowing I'd soon be home reliving my agonizing mistake. Rewind.

Play. Cry. Rewind. Eat ice cream. Cry. Repeat. And then suddenly, through the crowd, there she was. In her dress. Sitting in a chair side stage. Changing out of her heels into a pair of Uggs. "That's how you do it," I thought. "A fucking pro."

I caught her attention. "Thank you for coming," she said. "When I was young, people did that for me." She smiled and I smiled back, simultaneously thanking and apologizing to her. "I'm so sorry, Anita." She didn't seem bothered or upset. She slipped on the other boot and kept moving. Did she know what happened up there? Of course she did. I was grateful.

I went home, lay in my bed, and tried so very very hard to fall fast asleep.

Banana Walnut Chocolate Chip Muffins

INGREDIENTS (FOR 6 SMALL MUFFINS)

¼ cup [55 g] butter

2 very ripe bananas, mashed

1 large egg

½ cup [100 g] sugar

1 tsp vanilla extract

1 cup [140 g] all-purpose flour

½ tsp baking soda

Pinch of salt

½ cup [90 g] chocolate chips

½ cup [60 g] toasted walnuts

METHOD OF PREPARATION

1. Preheat the oven to 375°F (190°C). Grease six cups of a muffin tin or line with paper liners.

2. In a small microwave-safe bowl, melt the butter. Pour the melted butter into a medium mixing bowl and add the mashed bananas, egg, sugar, and vanilla.

3. In a separate bowl, mix the flour, baking soda, and salt.

4. Add the dry ingredients to the wet ingredients, add the chocolate chips and walnuts, and mix well. Divide the batter among the prepared muffin cups.

5. Bake for 15 to 20 minutes, or until a toothpick inserted into the center comes out clean.

Thank you.

Many people helped to make this book what it is, but the contributors who gave their time, heart, and memories to this project certainly top the list. Thank you for your effort and thoughtfulness; I am proud and grateful to have each of your stories in here.

A huge and heartfelt thank-you to all the colleagues, agents, assistants, and gatekeepers who made it possible to extract each of these stories and tolerated my many, many, many emails and thinly veiled pleading.

My immeasurable thanks to Jamie Thompson for the trust, guidance, and belief in my ideas all these years. Thank you to Vanessa Dina and everyone at Chronicle for their expertise and enthusiasm.

Thank you from the bottom of my heart to Grant Cornett, whose ability to find the optimism in melancholy and vice versa has kept my sensibility company for over twenty years. Your work was as much a point of inspiration as execution for this project.

To Ben Wagner, to whom I, almost literally, owe everything: From the title to the precision and rigor of all these pages, thank you for turning so much raw material into organized beauty.

To Ryan McLaughlin, who spilled a gallon of milk on the floor mat of his car during the hottest week of the summer and the week he tested these recipes, crystallizing our theme into perfect form: Thank you. I am lucky to have your friendship and talent on my side.

Thanks to Amy Wilson and Maggie Ruggiero for their skills and invention. Props to Ella Loudon for being the kind of person who plants her face in a cake with such style and confidence.

Thank you to Sam Wagner for the patience, efficiency, and actual skills to make some words into a book.

To Denny Agassi for your assistance, insight, and overall brilliance. You made this whole experience more fun and the result more potent.

Thanks to Sarah Hsia for making sure I dotted my i's and crossed my t's and didn't send myself to jail.

To Mariel Cruz, I can't thank you enough for your unmatched support, unflinching feedback, and unfailing friendship. Thank you to Emily Bernstein for being the best. And thank you to all the brainstormers and true believers who helped make this list of contributors what it is: Jason Rodgers, Paul Hamann, Jane Gladstein, Tchaiko Omowale, Kelly McCabe, Pam Nashel, Nicole Hegeman, Suzi Jones, Kim Holly, Avery Willis Hoffman, Jack DeBoe, Andrea Clemente, Mason Pettit, and Weyland Southon.

Thank you to the people who kept and keep me going: David Riley, Joan Dolan, the Hothans, Tanya Lofgren & Delia Kurland, Sarah, Sam & Alex, the Thompsons, Ultimate Neighbors, John Mahoney, Tedd Patterson, the Johnson/Miners, Amee Gray, Rachel McPherson, Leila Zimbel, Rebecca Meek, the P floor, the Hurins, Samanta Fonseca, Erica Turett, and Mali Sicora. Thank you to the loves of my life, Solomon and Atticus. And to Meshell, whose recipes are the cure for so many of my life's disasters: Thank you, I love you beyond words.